# Student Revolt

Also available

# Student Revolt

## Voices of the
## Austerity Generation

Matt Myers

Introduction by Paul Mason

First published 2017 by Pluto Press
345 Archway Road, London N6 5AA

www.plutobooks.com

The Left Book Club, founded in 2014, company number 9338285 pays
homage to the original Left Book Club founded by Victor Gollancz in 1936.

British Library Cataloguing in Publication Data
A catalogue record for this book is available from the British Library

ISBN   978 0 7453 3734 0   Paperback
ISBN   978 1 7868 0160 9   PDF eBook
ISBN   978 1 7868 0162 3   Kindle eBook
ISBN   978 1 7868 0161 6   EPUB eBook

# Contents

# Series Preface

The first Left Book Club (1936–48) had 57,000 members, had distributed two million books, and had formed 1,200 workplace and local groups by the time it peaked in 1939. LBC members were active throughout the labour and radical movement at the time, and the Club became an educational mass movement, remodelling British public opinion and contributing substantially to the Labour landslide of 1945 and the construction of the welfare state.

Publisher Victor Gollancz, the driving force, saw the LBC as a movement against poverty, fascism, and the growing threat of war. He aimed to resist the tide of austerity and appeasement, and to present radical ideas for progressive social change in the interests of working people. The Club was about enlightenment, empowerment, and collective organisation.

The world today faces a crisis on the scale of the 1930s. Capitalism is trapped in a long-term crisis. Financialisation and austerity are shrinking demand, deepening the depression, and widening social inequalities. The social fabric is being torn apart. International relations are increasingly tense and militarised. War threatens on several fronts, while fascist and racist organisations are gaining ground across much of Europe. Global warming threatens the planet and the whole of humanity with climate catastrophe. Workplace organisation has been weakened, and social democratic parties have been hollowed out by acceptance of pro-market dogma. Society has become more atomised, and mainstream politics suffers an acute democratic deficit.

Yet the last decade has seen historically unprecedented levels of participation in street protest, implying a mass audience for progressive alternatives. But socialist ideas are no longer, as in the immediate post-war period, 'in the tea'. One of neoliberalism's achievements has been to undermine ideas of solidarity, collective provision, and public service.

The Left Book Club aspires to meet this ideological challenge. Our aim is to offer high-quality books at affordable prices that are carefully selected to address the central issues of the day and to be accessible to a wide general audience. Our list represents the full range of progressive traditions, perspectives, and ideas. We hope the books will be used as the basis of reading circles, discussion groups, and other educational and cultural activities relevant to developing, sharing, and disseminating ideas for change in the interests of the common people at home and abroad.

The Left Book Club collective

# *Acknowledgements*

I would like to thank Achille Marotta, Charlotte Grace, Suyin Haynes, Mark Bergfeld, Nick Evans and Jonas Liston for helping with the project.

# List of Abbreviations

| | |
|---|---|
| AUT | Association of University Teachers |
| BIS | Department for Business, Innovation and Skills |
| CACHE | Cambridge Academic Campaign for Higher Education |
| CLASSE | Association pour une solidarité syndicale étudiante. ASSÉ, and its large coalition CLASSE, is a Canadian student union |
| EAN | Education Activist Network |
| NCAFC | National Campaign Against Fees and Cuts |
| NEC | National Executive Committee (NUS) |
| NUS | National Union of Students |
| PFI | Private Finance Initiative |
| RMT Union | Rail and Maritime Workers Union |
| SNP | Scottish National Party |
| SOAS | School of Oriental and African Studies |
| SWP | Socialist Workers Party |
| TSG | Territorial Support Group |
| TUC | Trades Union Congress |
| UAL | University of the Arts London |
| UCL | University College London |
| UCU | University Colleges Union |
| ULU | University of London Union |
| UWE | University of the West of England |

# Introduction

## Paul Mason

What struck me was the calmness. Indeed, the monotone. I'd been a student activist in the early 1980s: when we occupied Sheffield University we banged on the doors of the admin offices so hard, the staff burst into tears. Our debates had been fiery, male and about which kind of Marxism was right, what it meant to be subordinate to the proletariat. This was different.

I was in the occupation of the Brunel Gallery by students at SOAS. They didn't disrupt the functioning of the university. The debates were not really about the politics of the occupation. Indeed, they were not really debates: they were a series of monotone, highly qualified, suggestions, which people assented to by doing the twinkle gesture I'd seen in anti-capitalist-movement tent camps.

Then – to emphasise the distanced travelled in historical time – a lecturer with a grey beard and a leather jacket stood up to urge the students to be more radical. They politely ignored him and visibly flinched at the rhetorical inflexions his voice used to make his point.

At the end of the meeting, the facilitator – a young guy with a beard – called for consensus on whether to carry on. When everyone agreed he pronounced calmly: 'Good, my house is shit anyway.'

\* \* \*

When the global financial crisis broke in September 2008, we thought it might trigger a re-run of the 1930s. A smashed financial system, years of low growth and austerity ahead. But there were two big differences: the absence of an alternative ideology to free-market capitalism, and the absence of protest.

'Where are the protests?' journalists and politicos asked each other in the green rooms of major TV talk shows. Sure, there were some symbolic ones but, without an active and militant labour movement, it seemed we were about to experience the first depression era in the history of capitalism during which people would suffer quietly.

Then, in the autumn of 2009 students in California began to occupy buildings in protest at tuition fee hikes. It was not the action itself that was startling but the language and ideascape it generated. In their 'Communique from an Absent Future', students at UC Santa Cruz summed up a deep unease among the young at the marketisation of education.

> We work and we borrow in order to work and to borrow. And the jobs we work toward are the jobs we already have. Close to three quarters of students work while in school, many full-time; for most, the level of employment we obtain while students is the same that awaits after graduation. Meanwhile, what we acquire isn't education; it's debt. We work to make money we have already spent, and our future labor has already been sold on the worst market around.*

Three striking aspects in this text foreshadow the way the UK student protests would unfold, and underpin their significance.

* https://wewanteverything.wordpress.com/2009/09/24/communique-from-an-absent-future/

First, the dreamlike poetry of the language. This was a generation that had begun to understand, implicitly, what Guy Debord and the Situationists of 1968 had to work out theoretically: that action could be effective even when gestural and that language sometimes could do the job of a barricade.

Second, that the struggles of modern students are primarily economic – and yet their economic grievances challenge the validity of the system. The whole system is based on their underpaid work, they are part of the precariat – and, unlike my generation in the 1980s, were therefore not destined to play a mere subsidiary role to a bigger force, the working class.

Indeed, as one veteran of 1968 pointed out to me, as students surged down Whitehall in late November 2010, the numerical expansion of post-16 and university student numbers had now put a Situationist at around 50 per cent of family dinner tables. Students were no longer to be merely the 'detonator' for the explosive mass that was the working class: they were part of the explosive.

Third, that this was not merely an outbreak of unrest: it was a break in consciousness. Students had drunk the kool-aid of free-market economics; they had, of necessity, bought into the culture of individuality and competition, whereby everybody is tested every few months and accorded status via the results.

Now they realised it was all being done so they could get jobs as baristas, or unpaid roles as interns, or to rot on meagre pay and high debt in professional jobs whose benefits would never match what they had commanded in their parents' era.

So, when the UK student protest movement exploded on 10 November 2010, in the Millbank Tower riot, much of the ideology was already implicit and widespread.

My generation were genuinely amazed to find that power structures other than class could shape history. We had to discover Foucault, Fanon and Firestone – against the wishes and prejudices of our mentors on the left. In the student occupations of 2010 it was these authors whose books you repeatedly found scattered amid the sleeping bags. Marx not so much. Lenin and Trotsky not at all.

The trajectory of that movement is recounted in this book. From Millbank through to late November, the most striking fact was the involvement of estate-dwelling, migrant youth drawn into the protest by the parallel cancellation of a small weekly benefit known as EMA. It was they who turned the riots into serious violence, and they who brought their music – Dubstep and Grime – into the mass student gatherings.

It was they too who interacted with the undergraduates to produce a unique social media culture: not just Twitter and Facebook but the all-important Blackberry messaging service that would later feature prominently in the urban riots of Summer 2011.

For the student protest, the efficiency of social media and messaging apps was clear when a largely under-18-led protest descended from Nelson's Column in London down Whitehall, clashing with police. Groups of young people arrived from all over London on public transport, timing their arrival to within a 10-minute window and causing mayhem.

The 9 December riot in Parliament Square was the high-point of the movement, involving large numbers of under-18s and a massive mobilisation of university students, some of whom came wearing makeshift body armour, and ready to fight the police, who I watched at close quarters lose control, despite inflicting extreme violence on the protesters.

After that the movement was on a downward trajectory, but its long-term impacts still shape British politics.

First, a generation of students was radicalised in a wholly new way. Their implicit understanding of gesturality, the unavoidable economic core to their grievance, and the fact that this was a mass break in consciousness called to mind Hippolyte Taine's famous description of the lower middle class of France pre-1789.

Don't worry about the peasants, Taine advised nine-teenth-century France, on the basis of the 1789 experience. Worry about doctors, lawyers and clerks without clients; educated people starving in garrets – so many Robespierres and St Justs in waiting. What calls them into the sunlight, Taine warned, is when all the structures of the old society crumbled.

As I watched students surge around a marooned police van in Whitehall, it occurred to me that the process was being repeated: these graduates without a future were turning into 'Jacobins with a laptop'.

They were part of a wider global social phenomenon, which moved to different rules compared to the old proletariat and the old intelligentsia. This was, in fact, a revolt of the so-called networked individuals, the new sociological type called into being by the information society and assumed, until now, to be immune to protest and addicted to selfishness.

I observed young journalists discover a new and powerful voice as they dodged police batons. I heard some move from liberalism to anarcho-communism in weeks. And they displayed a resilience and a logicality young people are not supposed to possess. One told me: 'We've been tested to the limits of our ability inside the education system for every month during our entire lives. That breeds a lot of conformism, but once its broken the ruling class is going to find out it is dealing with a very professionalised, capable and determined group.'

It was the core group of thinkers and protesters from late 2010 that went on to stage anti-government riots in 2011, the UK Uncut movement and the Occupy London Stock Exchange camp, which became part of the global Occupy movement in September 2011.

After that, via the various routes of alternative journalism, climate activism, Palestinian solidarity, refugee campaigns and trade union organising, the Class of the Millbank 2010 Riot effectively became the core of the movement that would put Jeremy Corbyn into the leadership of the Labour Party. They were to be found, by Spring 2017, in core positions of the Momentum movement inside the Labour Party, or in relatively senior roles in mainstream and alternative left journalism.

By now, many of the core concepts we used to try to understand the 2010 student movement are accepted in political science. The student as economic lynchpin for neoliberal jobs market; the importance of social media in destroying the elite's means to transmit and create ideology; the understanding of non-violence as a core tactic.

So, it is worth reiterating that these were new and shocking factors in 2010, which required some sorting through and theorising.

The British student protests of 2010 were part of a wider global upswing which coalesced into a systemic critique of neoliberal capitalism. The most striking aspect of this wider movement was its conscious deployment of horizontal structures to prevent the emergence of hierarchy and patriarchy along the lines twentieth-century revolutionaries had assumed were natural.

Following key participants from the UK student movement, as 2010 turned into 2011, I was stunned to see two of them tweeting from Cairo on the 'day of the camels' – a critical moment in Egypt's revolution. Soon veterans of the Californian occupations would show up in Tel Aviv's tent camp; Spanish students who'd lived through the London clashes were among those who sat down at the Puerta del Sol in Madrid on 15 May. Greek left-wing academics running a blog called Occupied London were suddenly writing about the occupation of their own country's main square.

Ultimately, what the protests produced were two lasting legacies: an international network of people who understood both the methods of horizontal protest and their limitations; and an embedded sense that the neoliberal system needs to be replaced.

Ironically the issue of university tuition fees, which sparked the 2010 protest, has now become the major point of disagreement between the pro-capitalist wing of Labour and the Corbyn leadership.

Corbyn chose to include the complete scrappage of tuition fees in the June 2017 Labour general election manifesto despite the fact that it would create the biggest single price tag of the entire programme – £11 billion – and that it meant abandoning an implicit promise to roll back welfare cuts.

Corbyn calculated – correctly – that behind the student cohort of 2010 – many of them now professionals in their late 20s – stand seven more cohorts who understand the injustice of high tuition fees. He calculated that this politicised generation would turn out in large numbers to vote, on a scale not witnessed for three decades. He was right.

Now, by contrast, maintaining high-cost student debt has become the last-ditch defence line for Blairism within the Labour Party. As this book is published, the Labour right has chosen to make reversing Corbyn's commitment to scrap university fees its number one target.

The stories outlined in this book show why we must defend the principle of free university education. Information is the raw material of the next industrial revolution. The universally educated human being is its new proletariat. Tuition fees are, in this analogy, the equivalent of the indentured labour, gangmaster and discipline systems that workers endured in the first 30 years of the factory system.

Tuition fees were enacted in 1998 as a symbolic act of financialisation: the replacement of mutual social obligations with credit obligations. The fight for free university education is the issue that woke a generation of individualists and conformists out of their slumbers. Its achievement, within 10 years, would mark their rite of passage from the edges of politics to its centre.

June 2017

# CHAPTER ONE

# *Revolt*

The student revolt that erupted in November 2010 was one of the most radical in British history. Hundreds of thousands of students – organising themselves outside traditional party or student union structures – walked out of classes, took to the streets, and occupied their universities. Out of apathy and disengagement came the forcible entry of a new generation onto the stage of British politics. The demonstrations sent shockwaves through the heart of the British establishment. The police, newspapers and government were caught unawares. Fighting the proposed tripling of tuition fees and the cuts to Educational Maintenance Allowance (EMA), students posed the first and most serious challenge to the Coalition government's agenda of austerity. The 'austerity generation' was made not as a victim of unjust policies, but in resistance to them. This book is the story of that movement told through the voices of those who made it.

The year 2010 represented a 'widening of the field of possibility', as Jean-Paul Sartre wrote of 1968.[1] No student movement in British history had so openly flouted the rules of political engagement. No student movement had ever caused such a 'public order' crisis, nor been met with such severe police repression. Not since the Iraq War had such a powerful social movement emerged on Britain's streets. Never had a movement been so representative of the student body, nor possessed so strong a case for their demands. Never had there been such a radical potential for linking students struggling against fees and cuts with others resisting austerity. Never had the opportunity to politicise a whole generation been so cruelly missed.

The movement was unsuccessful in defeating the government's plans, thwarted by the intransigence of the Coalition. Like those in 1968, the rulers in 2010 also outlasted the student revolt. David Cameron – like Richard Nixon, Georges Pompidou, Leonid Brezhnev and Edward Heath – was the ultimate victor. The government knew the movement was about more than fees and cuts in education. The *Financial Times* understood the significance of the stand-off with the students: without winning this first battle, the newspaper claimed, the Coalition would come unstuck when other groups were affected by austerity.[2] The students' spirit of resistance could spread.

The outcome of the movement did not diminish the profundity of the experience for those present. 'It is likely the class of 2010 will be marked forever by these events', *The Guardian* predicted. 'Perhaps, 40 years from now, this week's demos will be the subject of nostalgic documentaries and writings, as those of 1968 have recently been.'[3] Students in 2010 understood the historical significance of their actions. 'It was our '68', a participant in this book noted. 'We felt like we were changing the world', said another.

There is nothing new about student protest in Britain. Yet the 2010 revolt was to be more passionate and intense because of its rarity. The revolt challenged stereotypes. Networked forms of online communication allowed the twenty-first-century student protest to be simultaneously local and global.[4] French onlookers watched in amazement as British students performed their month-long *jacquerie*. The French student movement had a more developed tradition of direct action and a history of victories. In 2006, students had successfully united with workers to prevent the *Contrat Premiere Embauche* (CPE) law that stripped young people of many of their workers' rights. Occupations occurred at 90 universities, with 3 million people taking to the streets.[5] In Paris for part of the 2010 movement, Malia Bouattia recounts how French students were shocked when they saw 'these otherwise quiet, tame people that usually just queue for the sake of queuing, ... suddenly ... kicking off due to the tripling of fees'. Paul Mason watched a young man address the SOAS occupation:

One man, a young Syrian, stood up to say: 'What we're doing here is having a global impact. This French journalist came up to me and said, this is amazing, this never happened before. What are the Brits doing? I said – what, you think the French are the only ones who can riot?'[6]

The government was afraid of 'contagion' from the continent. In 1968, the British student protests had been tame in comparison to those in France, Italy, Germany, Japan, and the United States. 'There is no memory of revolution in modern Britain', noted a leading activist from the time.[7] The discrepancy between the image of passive British students and the images shown on television screens in late 2010 encouraged a feeling of rupture.

The 2010 student revolt was one instance in a wider set of global anti-establishment struggles. The movement was indelibly stamped by the fallout from the 2008 financial crisis. Movements of the streets rather than revolts through the ballot box offered the chief means of articulating a collective grievance. From the student protests to the 2011 London riots, from Occupy to the Arab Spring, things were 'kicking off everywhere'.

The student movement of 2010 showcased new political, economic, social, communicative and technological developments. Movements of the streets provided laboratories for new and liberating uses of social media. Students outmanoeuvred traditional political organisations and experimented with new modes of political practice. New social subjects emerged, spontaneously organising themselves from below and building through old and new networks. University students defending public education mobilised with college students defending a weekly grant (EMA) to help poorer students stay in college. 'There was a generational un-channelled anger out there', remembered college student Kieran Sutton.[8] The spectre of the 'graduate without a future' united with youth from the 'slums of London' hung over Britain in late 2010.

The abruptness of the revolt laid waste the assumption of youth apathy – of a 'jilted generation' incapable of political interest, collective action or common purpose. Students posed fundamental questions of justice and fairness to a political class unaccustomed to open defiance. Complacently assuming that student unrest had been vanquished, the government looked on as students transformed themselves from passive consumers of education into founders of a radical movement. Youth alienation from politics and the political process had been decades in the making. One researcher claimed the 'millennials' were the most apathetic generation in British history.[9] The electoral promises of all parties – Liberal Democrats, Conservatives and Labour – were broken so brazenly, and with such little chance of recourse, that the students had no one to represent them but themselves.

Having lamented youth disengagement from politics for decades, when faced with a real movement of young people, Britain's political class closed ranks. According to Nick Clegg, young people had failed to see the 'true picture'.[10] According to David Cameron, their passion was 'drowning out' the truth.[11] 'I would feel ashamed if I didn't deal with the way that the world is, not simply dream of the way the world I would like it to be', Clegg lectured the 'dreamer' students who challenged him on his broken promise on fees.[12] Forgive the young, the Coalition cried, for they know not what they do. Cameron refused to have his youthful 'one-nation' idealism usurped by the students: 'We've seen the protests. We've seen the marches. We've seen how passionate many of our students are about this issue. Well let me tell you this: I am just as passionate.'[13]

The government's plans were intended to increase students' choice over their education and to make institutions more receptive to student needs. 'My principle was: what is in the best interests of young people, given the public spending constraints?', argued Minister for Universities and Science, David Willetts. When students demanded a different path, they were forcibly detained in areas known as 'kettles', charged with horses and pilloried in the press. More than just a movement to defeat the fee rise, the students were challenging the government's right to rule, and political parties' right to break their electoral promises. Worst of all, from the government's perspective, the students were unable to comprehend their own best interests. Students were flagrantly disputing the 'TINA' ideology – that *there is no alternative.*

Unable to countenance a movement that so openly contradicted their claim to speak for the student interest, the government treated the protests as a problem of public order. The Coalition government pathologised its unruly challengers as violent agitators led by foreign elements, intent on sullying the war dead and threatening the Royal Family. One Conservative MP, Julian Lewis, compared the students to 'foreign preachers'.[14] Theresa May praised this 'cleverly linked' analogy between the students and threats posed by the 'War on Terror'.[15] The British state remained ever vigilant against threats posed by enemies from within and without.

The students were confronted with vitriol and condescension in equal measures. Before the 2010 movement took off, a leading journalist had told students that there were more important people in society to be worried about.[16] 'Boys and girls' were playing out their 'St Trinian's riots', claimed one *Daily Mail* columnist.[17] A leader article for *The Times* argued that 'within every student body there are small left-wing cliques who believe in violent direct action ... They just wanted to run around in front of the television cameras saying: "Look at me, aren't I clever?" No, not really.'[18] 'The truth', a columnist for *The Guardian* noted, is that adults 'are too wise to waste their energy on something so silly' as challenging austerity: 'Protesting against the cuts is like protesting against water's stubborn habit of flowing downwards.'[19] 'There are swings of emotions in politics', noted David Willetts in his interview: 'Things aren't just people rationally calculating if a policy was fair and progressive or not.' With precious few exceptions, students had few friends in the mainstream media or in the political class willing to give a voice to those in the streets.

The condescension of politicians and journalists makes E.P. Thompson's concept of the 'moral economy of the crowd' all the more important for understanding the revolt. Thompson defined a 'moral economy' as a complex set of attitudes and norms of justice present within a historically discrete social group. Like other historians of social movements, Thompson refused to countenance that the movements of the English poor were irrational, uninformed and bereft of logic. So too the 2010 student generation had to overcome the haughty pathologising from those with power and influence. The students were a 'feral' mob, according to David Cameron, and enmeshed with 'malevolent forces' according to one MP.[20] But understanding the protestors as logical, informed, conscious of their interests and with a sophisticated conception of justice is as critical for the 2010 generation as it was for those in Thompson's study.

One of the movement's notable features was that most of the student protesters wouldn't be affected by the fee increases. This often went unacknowledged by Coalition politicians. Unlike in continental Europe, fee increases would only effect new entrants into higher education – leaving out all those already studying for their degrees. Thompson's eighteenth-century crowd rioted for a 'just price' for bread, just as British students rioted to assert their own 'moral economy' of education. The 'mobs' carrying out 'popular direct action' – be they students at Millbank or bread rioters in the late eighteenth century – have behind them 'some legitimising notion of right'.[21] As Thompson writes:

It is possible to detect in almost every eighteenth-century crowd action some legitimising notion. By the notion of legitimation I mean that the men and women in the crowd were informed by the belief that they were defending traditional rights or customs; and, in general, that they were supported by the wider consensus of the community.[22]

Such popular conceptions of justice made the student revolt more than a movement against fees and cuts. Young people were defending the values of the 'commons' – of a future without debt, where education would not be a commodity to be bought and sold.

Those students not cowed by parliamentary defeat and police repression took their experience into new projects. The history of UK Uncut – a protest group which put the question of tax avoidance onto the agenda of British politics – is indelibly linked to the student movement. The 2010 generation participated in the 2011 London riots, organised solidarity with the public sector strikes in November 2011, founded the Radical Independence Campaign in Scotland, and took part in the 'surge' into the Green Party before the 2015 general election. They would also play important roles in the campaign to elect and re-elect Jeremy Corbyn as Labour Party leader, as well as in the party's unexpected success in the June 2017 election.

When the student movement of 2010 ended is a point of debate amongst its participants. For some it was the vote on the 9th of December 2010. For others, it came after the TUC-organised march on 26th of March 2011. That the movement didn't continue past the 21st of November 2012 is not contested. On this day an NUS-organised rally at Kennington Park in south London ended in mud, freezing rain and an invasion of the speakers' platform. In an irony lost on those drenched and demoralised, the student movement of 2010 was buried in the same place (and in the same dreary rain) as the Chartists – the great democratic movement of the nineteenth century – had been, on the 10th of April 1848.

Participants looked back on their experiences as profoundly liberating. For them, the movement became a liminal space that broke with the strictures of what Mark Fisher called 'capitalist realism'.[23] Whether or not that was the case, they were certainly openly flouting '*austerity realism*' – the assumption that there was no alternative to austerity. 'The only thing I can compare the current situation with is emerging from a state of deep depression', Fisher wrote of the 2010 movement:

There's the rush that you get ... the occasional lurching anxieties, a sense of how precarious it all seems ... and yet not only is it maintaining itself, it's proliferating, intensifying, feeding on itself – it's impossible, but it's happening – the reality programme resetting itself.[24]

It was this asymmetry with the times that made the 2010 generation so exceptional.

Though defeated, the students showed that mass movements in an age of austerity were possible and necessary. The student revolt laid the basis for the leftward shift amongst young voters at the June 2017 general election. On 8 June 2017, an electoral 'youthquake' saw an estimated 60 per cent of those aged 18 to 24 vote for Corbyn's Labour Party in the largest youth turnout since 1992.[25] This growth in politicisation did not emerge from nowhere. The 2010 student movement was the first to expose the growing generational cleavage that has now gripped British politics. The political class chose to ignore its warnings and are now living with the consequences.

Young voters in 2017, like the protesters in 2010, refused to believe that there was no alternative to austerity. In the student revolt and the June 2017 general election, the austerity generation was made not as a victim of unjust policies, but in resistance to them. In both cases, young people chose to be the generation to *end* austerity. Both rejected worsening standards of living, debt and precarity. Both asserted that the misfortune of growing up after the 2008 financial crisis would not define their future. In 2010, young people chose to be the subjects of their political fate by taking to the streets; in 2017, they used the ballot box. Like those in 2010, the struggle of young people in 2017 is over who should pay for the economic crisis: the many or the few. The result at the general election shows how powerful a force this new political subject can be. To understand the radical changes to British politics since 2010, we need to start with the generation which came of age politically in that year.

## The political economy of the revolt

The headline issue that was to define the movement was the proposed rise in tuition fees. Commissioned under the Labour government by Peter Mandelson, and published in October 2010, the Browne Review advocated a transformed higher education system. Students were to face potentially unlimited fees set by universities, an expansion of government-guaranteed student loans, and the substantial marketisation of the higher education system through inter-university competition.[26] The Browne Review's one major suggestion that was not implemented by the Coalition government was limitless tuition fees. Universities were to be allowed to charge £6,000 a year in fees, with £9,000 being an 'exception' – although almost no university chose to charge less than £9,000. Students would not have to repay the government loans until they were earning more than £21,000 per year, when they would begin to pay the debt off at a rate of 9 per cent of all income over that threshold. After 2010, tuition fees in England became the highest in the world for public universities, with one of the highest interest rates for student loans.[27] The changes that were later described as putting 'students at the heart of the system' resulted in the largest student movement in Britain since the 1970s.[28]

Just over a week after the Browne Review was published, the government's Comprehensive Spending Review announced a 25 per cent reduction in public spending and a cut of 40 per cent to the higher education budget. The Chancellor George Osborne wanted to cut public spending by £81 billion to eliminate the deficit by 2015. The Coalition's proposals for education were designed to structurally transform higher education from a public, cultural good into what Stefan Collini has called a 'lightly regulated market in which consumer demand, in the form of student choice, is sovereign in determining what is offered by service providers'.[29] Higher education was to become a market, ceasing to be a public good paid for through public taxation. Like in any other market, students as consumers were to determine the service provision of universities. Competition was to be a tide that lifts all boats, to quote the oft-repeated phrase of Universities Minister David Willetts.[30]

The rise in fees, the education cuts and the marketisation of higher education were about more than competition, efficiency and choice. The reforms were intended to reshape student subjectivity. 'Economics are the method: the object is to change the soul', as Margaret Thatcher famously said. Traditionally, students had been seen by governments as barriers to the working of the market – popularly portrayed as either unproductive layabouts dependent on taxpayer cash or as ungrateful agitators who use their borrowed time to disrupt society. After the Browne Review, however, students were to become the vessels for storming one of the last bastions of British civil society to have remained outside total market discipline. The reforms would create a self-generating market ideology, integrating hitherto politically dangerous and unprofitable sectors (students) into both market relations and a longer-term regime of labour discipline (ensured through vast levels of debt). The plans came unstuck when students refused to pay for a crisis not of their making.

Students felt deeply betrayed by the Liberal Democrats – the party which for years had campaigned to abolish tuition fees. In their manifesto they had promised to 'scrap unfair university tuition fees so everyone has the chance to get a degree, regardless of their parents' income'.[31] Party leader Nick Clegg willingly went on camera promising to vote against any rise in fees. Every Liberal Democrat MP had signed an NUS pledge to stop the fee rise. The party manifesto promised to scrap fees immediately for all final year students, and to phase out fees for all students 'taking their first degree'. All this was to be done 'without cutting university income'.[32] This pledge enthused students. In February-March 2010 only 27 per cent of students had intended to vote for the Liberal Democrats, but by election day it was 48 per cent.[33] The betrayal of the

Liberal Democrat pledge became a symbol for the broken political contract between young people and the political class.

*A marketising tradition*

The Coalition government's reforms were not a rupture with the past, but furthered existing processes both inside and outside higher education. For decades, the British state has faced radical restructuring. Welfare provision has thinned, public services have been subjected to market discipline, and government resources have been transferred to make private firms more competitive. Under the government of Margaret Thatcher, spending on higher education was held down as part of a general attempt to reduce public expenditure. Tuition fees for British nationals were not an invention of the Coalition government. They had been proposed unsuccessfully in 1984 by Sir Keith Joseph, Conservative Secretary of State for Education. Students successfully fought the attempt to scrap the universal minimum grant and impose a means-tested fee of £520. An icy reaction from Vice Chancellors, an NUS campaign of nationally coordinated 24-hour 'sit-ins' at all institutions, and a Tory backbench rebellion, forced Joseph to back down.[34] Coming during Thatcher's ongoing confrontation with the miners, the government conceded.

It would take a Labour government to bring in a fee-paying system. Commissioned under John Major's Conservative government and published in 1997 after Labour had come to power, a report by the Dearing Commission recommended the introduction of a 'student contribution' in higher education, with an exemption for poorer students.[35] Under the governments of both Major and Tony Blair, the expansion of student numbers coincided with a reduction in the 'unit of resource'. The 'higher education unit of resource' – the amount of money spent by the government on each student's education – had been reduced by 25 per cent since 1989.[36] The report found public funding per student had halved in 18 years while student numbers had vastly increased. With the desire to see 50 per cent of those between the ages of 18 and 30 benefiting from some form of higher education by 2010, the Labour government aimed for 500,000 new university places by 2002. In practice, the expansion in numbers occurred with a corresponding fall in the money spent per student.[37] Blair's government was accused of 'wanting to increase participation without being willing to pay for it'.[38]

Before the 1997 election, Labour had promised not to institute top-up fees. In 1996, the Labour Students faction inside the NUS had 'urged the union to drop its support of free education to make things easier for Blair in the run-up to the election'.[39] As a reward for its fidelity, in 1998 a government bill scrapped maintenance grants and introduced upfront charges. 'We still believe that tuition fees are wrong in principle and practice', NUS President Andrew Pakes said.[40] Demonstrations continued. Protests in November 1998 included an occupation of the Department for Education and Employment, and a campaign of non-payment by six Oxford University students.[41] A 12,000-strong NUS march to Kennington Park in November 2000 was billed as 'the biggest student march for a decade'.[42] NUS President Owain James didn't sound a rousing note: 'Students are happy to contribute towards their education. But if you don't support those from the poorest background and you charge them £15,000 to go to university, then you will put them off.'[43] James, *The Guardian* reported, was more interested in opening up online marketing aimed at students, and achieving 'a slightly better deal on their mobile phones and bus tickets', than in tuition fees.[44] Students weren't able to prevent or reverse the £1,000 per year means-tested (and upfront) tuition fees and the scrapping of the £1,710 grant.[45] A Labour government had succeeded in bringing in fees and the increased marketisation of universities where Margaret Thatcher and John Major had failed.

The next fee rise came in 2004. Again, the 2001 Labour manifesto had promised not to introduce 'top-up' fees. Yet in January 2003, less than two years later, the party published a White Paper advocating that universities charge fees of up to £3,000 a year (by 2010 they would reach £3,290). In 2002, Labour's Education Secretary had told students 'there is no such thing as a free lunch'.[46] The higher fees were introduced in order to even out the 'graduate premium' – the surplus income graduates receive due to the increased earning potential provided by their degrees. In 2003, the Education Secretary and former NUS President Charles Clarke announced plans for variable top-up fees. These would be repayable after graduation, replacing the up-front tuition fee for students in England. 'Countries throughout the world have discovered', Clarke told the House of Commons, that 'requiring students to contribute to the cost of their education is the only realistic alternative'.[47] However, in the same year in Quebec a strike by 230,000 students (nearly half of the total student body) forced a halt in government cuts and secured an additional $70m funding pledge.[48] One year later, a social-democratic government in Germany was pushed to abolish fees on a state by state basis after large student protests.[49] The NUS's position was ambiguous, with it being unwilling to articulate a political alternative to the new fee system. Even though opinion polls at the time showed 59 per cent opposed the introduction of university top-up fees, the mass of students were not involved in opposing them.[50] A protest involving 31,000 students was organised by the NUS on the 26th of October 2003, but still the government persevered.[51] On the 27th of January 2004, Labour's imposition of top-up fees narrowly passed through Parliament with 316 votes for the bill and 311 against. Among the 72 Labour Party rebels stood Jeremy Corbyn and John McDonnell.

The bitter pill of top-up fees was sweetened with the introduction of the Educational Maintenance Allowance – a weekly grant of £30 a week introduced by the Labour government in 2004 to encourage students from families with an income less than £30,810 to continue into further education. A., a school student from south London who wished to remain anonymous, described why the EMA was so important:

> EMA was indispensable ... Growing up in a working-class background with a single mother who struggled in some cases to put food on the table, on top of things like stationery and books. Being able to go to school, equipped and prepared – that's what EMA stood for.

When the grant was abolished in early 2011, 647,000 under-18 year olds were recipients. Cuts to the EMA drove many school and college students to unite with the university students in 2010.

The Labour government were trailblazing where no other party dared to go. In May 2003, the Conservative Party leader, Iain Duncan Smith, pledged to abolish fees under a Tory government. He even attended the October 2003 NUS demonstration, but confined himself to '40 minutes of chatting to students in a pub'.[52] As the government's reforms became entrenched, political attitudes started to change. In 2008, the NUS – tailing the Conservative Party and David Cameron, who had recently changed the party's policy on free education – dropped their opposition to tuition fees.[53] David Willetts noted that there was 'an anxiety, and an understandable anxiety, especially under Michael Howard, that low income students were going to be put off [higher education]. But the evidence that came in from Blair was that they weren't being put off – because they weren't paying up front … That is what really shifted our thinking – the anxieties had been misplaced.' Wes Streeting, the new NUS President, called for a 'more pragmatic approach'.[54] Under the Labour government, private sector activity in higher education – exemplified in new Private Finance Initiative (PFI) schemes and the expansion of degree-awarding powers to private companies – grew from 32.3 per cent of all higher education spending in 2000 to 64.2 per cent in 2007.[55] This stood well above the EU average of 20.6 per cent.[56] It was under Labour in 2009 that provision for the university system was integrated into the Department for Business, Innovation and Skills (BIS). As Willetts noted, the new fee levels were 'conceptually the same model [as under Blair]. The graduate repayment scheme was essentially the one Blair designed, but instead pushed out much further.' The tripling of fees in 2010, the largest ever fee rise in world history, did not emerge from nowhere.

## The fire last time

The 2010 student movement stands in a long tradition of young people fighting for their rights in Britain. Although the mid 1980s represented a turning point, student politics did not disappear. Studies on British student movements has been heavily focused on the 1960s and '70s. There is an abundant literature on the student movements of 1968, across continental Europe and North America, especially oral histories. As noted earlier, in comparison to what took place in Italy, Germany, France and the US, Britain's 1968 was a tame affair: 'There were no barricades, no petrol bombs, no fire hoses, no tear gas, no heavy rioting, no national university strikes or general strikes, no mass destruction of property and no shootings.'[57] In Italy, France and Germany police violence 'acted as a trigger for further student support as more moderate students reacted not to the initial reason for student action but to repression by authorities'.[58] The riot – into which the 2010 protests often descended – was largely absent in the British 1960s. What made 2010 special was that it surpassed the British 1968 in its brazen flaunting of established decorum and its challenge to the legitimacy of fees, austerity and the forces of public order.

But student protest didn't start in the 1960s – it began even with the first universities. Medieval European university records show students organising against poor food, lodgings and teaching.[59] In medieval Italy, the University of Bologna faced the first ever lecture boycotts against poor teaching quality.[60] At the start of the nineteenth century, London medical students fought for new curriculum changes and better standards of teaching.[61] Yet by the early twentieth century, British students were not known for their progressive politics. The vast majority came from elite backgrounds, and after graduating entered into the higher echelons of the British state, the Empire or business. During the 1926 General Strike, university students from Oxford, Cambridge,

St Andrews, University College London, Edinburgh and Exeter, volunteered to act as strike breakers.[62] Things started to change in the early 1930s as a university-based anti-war movement emerged. This, combined with student support for the anti-fascists in the Spanish Civil War, the labour movement in Britain, and the formation of new socialist student societies, signalled the changes to come.[63] However, before the 1950s, universities and further education were the preserve of (male) children of the elite classes. Progressive movements were still confined to small minorities.

In the mid twentieth century, higher education faced its most radical transformation. The massive expansion in student numbers indelibly changed the student body's political character. In 1939 there were just 50,000 students in higher education,[64] having increased from around 7,500 in 1900.[65] After the Second World War, the Labour Prime Minister Clement Attlee saw the rapid expansion of funding for further and higher education, and 'trained men and women in the various departments of our national life', as part of a solution to 'our post-war problems'.[66] The expansion in student numbers following the 1944 Butler Act matched the transformation in capitalism over the same period. A new mass service sector required different forms of education – especially generalised information processing and comprehension skills, and vocational qualifications in sciences and engineering. The post-war expansion of universities in the 1950s and 1960s was boosted by the Robbins Report of 1963, which stated that any 18 year old with adequate qualifications would be given the opportunity to attend higher education. By 1972, 14.2 per cent of the population was now entering full-time higher education.[67] From the 1970s, however, the

British state began redefining universities as business-like institutions operating in the interests of the national economy. A harbinger of the twenty-first century university can be found in the 'Warwick University Ltd' described by E.P. Thompson in 1970.[68] Academics and lecturers were increasingly pressured to produce 'value for money' in their teaching and to demonstrate, through a range of audit exercises, that their labour was worthy of public investment.

The year 1967 marked a turning point in student activism in Britain. This was the first year in which a mass movement of students marched *for themselves* as a discrete social group, and for their rights *as students* against the university. 'For the first time, British students showed collective solidarity in their role as students', Gareth Stedman Jones noted two years later.[69] The occupation, demonstrations and sit-ins by LSE students in 1967 against the appointment of Walter Adams – who had been implicated in the white-supremacist regime in Rhodesia – as university director led to protracted struggles over a series of grievances relating to the student experience. Students had been a social group 'in themselves', but after 1967 they had shown they could also act 'for themselves' as students. Partly led by the Conservative Party affiliated student union President, the movement included the 'Daffodil March' on the 17th of March 1967, where 2,000 LSE students marched down Fleet Street to protest the suspension of two protest leaders, carrying the infamous banner: 'Down with the Pedagogic Gerontocracy'. Although solidarity work with liberation struggles around the world hadn't ceased – the war in Vietnam played a critically galvanising role – students had paved the way for the defence of their own rights using radical new forms of direct action.

Precious little has been written on more recent cycles of protest. This lack of scholarship has fed popular conceptions that the '60s were an unprecedented and unrepeated period of sustained activism, followed only by political apathy.[70] The links between 2010 and 1968 were made largely by activists of the older generation and journalists recalling their youth. The 2010 protesters were the 'angelic spirits of 1968';[71] the UCL occupation was 'not exactly Paris 1968'.[72] 'They have arguably more to be angry about than my generation ... Some [of our] causes were indulgent', noted Brian Groom.[73] One journalist for the *Financial Times* went further:

> From the early 1960s to the late 1980s, occupying a library or scrimmaging with police was integral to the student lifestyle ... In the 1970s, a rioter would have worn a keffiyeh, both to conceal his identity from The Man and to channel the radical fashion chic of Yasser Arafat ... [Today] the protesters' cause is meanwhile too solipsistic to recapture the romantic radicalism of yore.[74]

The struggle of 2010 was more obviously economic and so less easily integrated into narratives of a 1968-reloaded. When describing itself, the 2010 generation talked of debt and of life prospects, not authoritarian and conservative culture. The slogan of the 1960s – 'Don't trust anyone over the age of 30' – didn't reappear in 2010. Parents were often allies in a collective defence of their education, not enemies. Rather than recreating the battles of previous generations, the 2010 generation was 'fighting against precarity, fearing debt, feeling dispossessed, and expressing understandable anger at the people making the decisions that affected their lives', as Nina Power argued. The struggle of the austerity generation was over which generation would pay for the 2008 economic crisis.

*Why oral history?*

The generation of 2010 was distrustful of external authority imposing prefabricated meanings onto its experiences. 'Out with the old politics', declared the writer Laurie Penny. Politicians were, she argued, 'making a fundamental error in assuming these young protesters want or need anybody to "be our voice"'.[75] Much like the 'New Left' of the 1960s, which stressed popular agency and consciousness in the making of history, participants in 2010 wanted to define their own movement. It is not a coincidence, noted the Italian oral-historian Alessandro Portelli, that 'oral history, at least in the shape it has taken in Italy, can be considered in many important respects a product of 1968'.[76] Much of the theorisation of 2010 came from outside the movement – from journalists and writers – rather than being retrospective intellectual production from inside.

For many of those interviewed here, I was a fellow-participant as well as an historian. Having been a school student in 2010, I am both close to and distant from the memories collected. The trust and mutual understanding fostered by the common experience of interviewer and interviewee provided a unique privilege, one which oral historians are often denied by their role as 'friendly neighbour and sympathetic outsider'.[77] 'The less the historians reveal about their identity and thoughts', Portelli wrote, 'the more likely informants are to couch their testimony in the broadest and safest terms, and to stick to the more superficial layers of their conscience and the more public and official aspects of their culture.'[78] Luisa Passerini described writing an oral history of Italy's 1968 student generation from the 'inside' in the following terms: 'The interviews plunge me into my own past: as I listen, the film of what I was doing at the time unreels.'[79] This close and intimate relationship to the subject matter poses its own problems. As Studs Terkel, the American oral historian, warned: 'You try to be objective but sometimes you become involved with the narrator.'[80] Proximity also opens up avenues that would be closed to 'outsiders'. A shared history between historian and correspondent can allow a more fruitful discussion of judgments, theories and explanations, as general descriptions of time and space are taken for granted.

No historian has previously attempted a history of the 2010 movement using the voices of participants. Of the three books that are based on, or include reference to, the movement, none engage in a serious attempt at an oral history or substantially root their analyses in first-hand experience.[81] The legacy of defeat overshadows the movement. Likewise, in the 1970s and '80s the 'counter-offensive' by the 'established order' also made accounting for the memory of the 1968 generation 'more problematic.'[82] Passerini's work on the generation of 1968 in Italy describes the pitfalls in the way of such an historical accounting: 'Memory redoubled in this way is hard to bear', she remembered while interviewing her contemporaries. 'It seems to me that until now no one has wanted to take on this burden, sometimes not even those who tell their stories.'[83]

Many participants' trajectories after the movement were hard to trace, making the historian's task more difficult. Those who have continued with activism, as well as those still embedded in friendship, social media and activist networks, or those with public profiles, have been easier to approach. The burden of collecting these memories is essential before they are lost forever. As Raphael Samuel noted, the oral historian's 'greatest contribution may well be in the collecting and safe preservation of his material rather than in the use he can immediately find for it'.[84] The current generation of movement activists are able to share their experiences and thoughts in real time on a multitude of online and offline platforms, experiences which in previous decades would have been left unrecorded. In an age of social media, a return to oral history might seem arcane. Yet one striking issue for historians of twenty-first century movements is the fragility of non-material sources. Many of the websites and online servers that hosted materials and discussions of the 2010 generation are now out of action, with their precious contents lost. Collecting the memories of those present prevents collective amnesia.

Oral historians of previous decades had to fight to have the discipline recognised by the rest of the historical profession. 'Oral history today', Eric Hobsbawm noted in the 1990s, 'is personal memory – which is a remarkably slippery medium for preserving facts.'[85] A.J.P. Taylor went further, dismissing oral history as but 'old men drooling about their youth'. Paul Thompson, one of the pioneers of British oral history, noted that the attitude of those opposed to oral evidence is

as much founded on feeling as on principle … Hence … the grasping of straws to justify their scepticism: usually a reminiscence about the inaccuracy of either their own or some other person's memory … [and] a fear of the social experience of interviewing, of the need to come out of the closet and talk to ordinary people.[86]

Critics of oral history are correct that the historian is never given an exact representation of the event, only memories of it. But, given the fallibility of memory, dates and narrative details can be checked against written sources. Furthermore, as Ronald Fraser argued in his oral history of the 1968 student generation in Europe and North America:

> What people felt (or more accurately, what today they remember having felt), what they hoped to achieve as much as what they in fact achieved, what should have happened and what would have been better if it had not happened, constitute historical facts as much as the events themselves.[87]

What people remember can tell us as much about events and their significance as the narrative of a newspaper article or data mined from a Twitter feed.

The driving force of this book is the voice of the participants, not that of the historian. The oral historian must be the chairperson of the debate that never happened. They must be the conscientious editor of experiences. This 'history-from-below' approach requires caution. As Passerini warned:

> Amongst the gravest of the inadequacies of oral history, I would suggest, is the tendency to transform the writing of history into a form of populism ... [which] runs the risk of constructing oral history as merely an alternative ghetto, where at last the oppressed may be allowed to speak.[88]

However, by including voices from all sides of the fees battle, as well as those from past movements, it is possible to counter the ghettoisation of experience. For the first time the NUS

President, the working-class college student, the government cabinet member, the revolutionary militant and the first-time protester can come together in dialogue. The inclusion of competing voices previously confined to their respective camps allows for an exploration in the contradictory assumptions of both. Students can now speak back to power where they had previously been kept out in the cold.

Oral history, as Portelli notes, is both an 'intellectual and … social endeavour'.[89] Both historian and interviewee come to a fuller understanding of their historical experience through recollection and interrogation. Subconscious memories become active and relevant anew. When interviewed for this book, the correspondents often became animated; their speech became quicker and more intense; images which had been blurred by time became vivid and alive. Those who had said 'Oh, I don't remember much' when they began, uncovered memories they thought had been consigned to oblivion. Feelings of power or emotion experienced in the past resurfaced, not as involuntary and individual memories, but as pieces of a still unwritten collective story. As Paul Thompson notes, 'oral history gives history back to the people in their own words; and in giving a past, it also helps them towards a future of their own making'.[90] History is never only the search for 'how things really were', but necessitates an openness to how things *might be*.

*Concepts*

The concept of 'generation' is central to the project. For commentators, the notion played a central role in 2010.[91] Since Karl Mannheim's essay, 'The Problem of Generations', the concept has developed and transformed into a category prevalent in both academic and popular discourse.[92] From the 'baby boomers' born after the Second World War, Generation X born during the late 1960s and 1970s, to the 'millennials', generations have become, for better or worse, symbolic markers of historical change. This book uses two generational markers: the 'austerity generation' and the 'Millbank generation'. The 'austerity generation' was formed by fate in circumstances outside their control, becoming adults after the 2008 financial crisis. With the Millbank generation, the austerity generation refused its label and demanded a different future. In the student revolt the Millbank and austerity generation were present simultaneously. The Millbank generation – a generation in revolt – reminds us that the austerity generation was not inevitable but contingent.

Some age cohorts will always be more 'generational' than others. The cohort of 2010 in large part understood themselves as a generation, but this wasn't unanimous. Common experience and generational identification are not necessarily mutually constitutive. What instead emerges from their voices is a similar emotive relationship with the movement itself. Many felt gratitude to the movement for making them the people they are. 'I'm so grateful for 2010' noted one contributor from the Cambridge occupation. Those participants who identified with the 'Millbank generation' are above all united in an emotional community, linked by the shaping experience of the 2010 movement.

The term 'student movement' needs elaborating. Ever since the 1960s, the sociological and political character of students and their movements have been a persistent concern for activists. 'Students, unlike workers, do not constitute a class.

The situation of the working class is a permanent one – it is a life situation', Gareth Stedman Jones argued in *Student Power* in 1969.[93] A methodological distinction between a movement in which students participate and a movement *of* students to assert or defend their rights *as* students is useful. As an example of the latter, 2010 exemplifies how a transitional social community – a cohort of those enrolled in school, college or university – organised themselves to assert their rights collectively in a unity greater than the sum of its parts.

### Final remarks

The interviews were conducted between September 2015 and January 2017. Responding to the same set of questions, interviewees discussed their experiences before, during and after the movement. The structure of the book matches this chronological approach. Chapter 2 begins with the mythic conception of the 2010 student movement: the 'Millbank demonstration' on November 10th. Chapter 3 interrogates the expectations of students and politicians in 2010, and how these changed as the movement progressed. Chapter 4 traces the radical street movement that engulfed British towns and cities for a month after November 10th. Chapter 5 focuses on the question of the movement's organisation, including the university occupations, and the role of political organisations and the NUS. Chapter 6 explores one of the most pressing questions of the book: why did the students lose? The concluding chapter focuses on the major themes of the revolt, and how the higher education reforms since 2010 have affected students' experience. The lessons of the movement for the current generation of students are discussed through the voices of current student activists.

Walter Benjamin wrote that 'memory is not an instrument for surveying the past but its theatre'. Memory, he continues,

> is the medium of past experience, just as the earth is the medium in which dead cities lie buried. He who seeks to approach his own buried past must conduct himself like a man digging. Above all, he must not be afraid to return again and again to the same matter; to scatter it as one scatters earth, to turn it over as one turns over soil.[94]

This book seeks to be such an excavation into memory. It aims, above all, to rescue an important moment in British history from the condescension of posterity. Hopefully future generations organising for a different world will find these memories useful.

# CHAPTER TWO

# *Millbank*

'This is the biggest workers' and students' demonstration in decades. It just shows what can be done when people get angry. We must build on this.'

John McDonnell MP[1]

The British student revolt was born at Millbank. The National Union of Students estimated that 52,000 students and lecturers marched through central London against increased tuition fees and funding cuts. The demonstration on the 10th of November 2010 did not go to plan. Exiting the planned route after Parliament, protestors occupied the headquarters of the Conservative Party in Millbank Tower. The demonstration set British politics alight for over a month. It's spontaneous radicalism and willingness to break barriers of legality makes it one of the most important British student demonstrations in history. It challenged the stereotype of the apathetic youth, disinterested in politics, and rebuffed the consensus that there were no dissenters to austerity.

Journalists often use the word 'Millbank' when talking about power in British politics. Perched on the banks of the Thames, Millbank Tower lies at the heart of the British establishment. Political parties, media studios and lobbying firms all tussle for proximity to Westminster. After November

10th 'Millbank' was to 'acquire another meaning', wrote Paul Mason. 'Millbank was where they lost control. The Coalition lost control of the political agenda; the NUS lost control of the student movement; the police lost control of the streets.'[2] The occupation of a ruling political party's headquarters shouldn't happen in any society, let alone in a member country of the G8. The symbolism of the occupation of Millbank Tower is critical to understanding the subsequent revolt.

Journalists argued that the demonstration was intimately related to upcoming rounds of austerity under the new government. The next day *The Times* front page announced that 'with the Coalition government six months old today, ministers are watching for any sense that the disorder represents a change of mood, with demonstrators trying to emulate the violence that has swept France and Greece'. The occupiers of Millbank Tower 'claimed to be acting in solidarity with public-sector workers and other groups affected by spending cuts'.[3] According to *The Guardian*, the demonstrators became 'a lightning rod for wider public unease with the government's public spending strategy'.[4] The protesters who had scaled the roof of Millbank Tower released a statement by text message quoted in *The Times*: 'This is only the beginning of the resistance to the destruction of our education system and public services.'[5]

The government agreed that the significance of the protest lay well outside higher education. It called into question the whole agenda of austerity. One government source said after the demonstration: 'This is just the beginning. This is the first of a series of protests by various sections of society against what we are doing. The problem is this sets the benchmark for other protests. We've got the union demos coming down the line.'[6] A spokesman for the Reuben Brothers, the owners of Millbank Tower, predicted the damage was 'likely to be thousands of pounds'.[7] Through twenty-first-century 'propaganda of the deed', British students had sent shockwaves to the heart of the British establishment.

The demonstration was organised jointly by the NUS and the Universities and Colleges Union (UCU) under the slogan 'Fund Our Future: Stop Education Cuts' and 'Demo-lition 10.11.10' – a (subsequently ironic) play on 'demo' and 'Coalition'. The then NUS President, Aaron Porter, was afraid the demonstration would garner too little, rather than too much, press coverage: 'There had been nothing in recent memory that would have given us cause to think there would be anything like the scale we saw in Millbank Tower … we should have anticipated something a little less peaceful.'

A demonstration of 25,000 students in Dublin two weeks earlier, over a rise in university registration fees, had descended into violence.[8] Few expected similar scenes in London. Clare Solomon, then President of the University of London Union (ULU), recounted that she 'wasn't privy to any plans to occupy Millbank … the meetings we had before the demonstrations in student union bars discussed how to get numbers on demonstrations and internal NUS politics … None of those meetings could claim to have organised 2010.' Vicki Baars, then NUS LGBT Officer and a National Executive Committee (NEC) member, remembered the constant phone-banks, distributing promotional materials and organising the demonstration's LGBT block (which had the dress code, 'builders'). 'I don't think Millbank was as orchestrated or planned as some people like to think', she recalled.

The feeder march that assembled outside ULU on Malet Street set off at noon to join the main part of the demonstration. By 2 p.m., 50,000 students and lecturers were on the move from Trafalgar Square to Millbank. The size of the demonstration shocked the NUS staff stewarding the demonstration as well as the police. Vicki Baars remembers 'seeing the look on the faces of the NUS staff like: "Is this ever going to end? There are so many people here."' Both the student activists and the police had to respond to a new protest climate in which social media was as important as the number of buses in predicting protest numbers. As Clare Solomon observed: 'These days with social media, Facebook and so on, when people organise, it's not always through the official union channels with coaches and things, and you don't always know the numbers.'

The official march was led by the 'Liberation' campaigns of the NUS – the Black Students', Women's and LGBT fractions. The Disabled Students' campaign set the pace of the demonstration. For Nina Power, a lecturer at Roehampton University and a columnist for *The Guardian*, the march looked much older than the later demonstrations. It was 'initially a formal march', she recalled, 'there was a lot of lecturers, teachers, school kids and students'. For Clare Solomon, the march was 'rather lively, it was rather angry … not full force kind of angry yet, as the NUS, given their kind of fairly liberal, you know, apolitical sort of approach, tried to dampen any sort of sit-downs and spiky actions'. Ben Beach, an architecture student at University College London, described the start of the demonstration as almost 'joyful', as police and protestors tried to outmanoeuvre each other. 'Even the cops were smiling – it was quite joyful.' This feeling was not to last.

A small group of student demonstrators attempted to occupy the Department for Business, Innovation and Skills – the government department responsible for instituting the rise in fees. Matt Cole, a Masters student in Philosophy at Kingston University who had just moved from the United States, was at BIS during the short-lived attempted occupation, having followed a friend 'connected to the anarchist and squatting scene'. At BIS 'it all kicked off for a bit, then riot police cut it off', he recalled. Also outside the revolving doors of BIS was Charlotte Grace, who had just graduated from architecture school. She was knocked unconscious by a police baton and dragged to safety.

Many smaller 'crews' started to send messages through the crowd. Gupt Singh recalled the 'very strange experience of some of the anarchists handing out little slips of paper ... I say leaflets, they were hardly like a single line of A4, just saying look out for the flare, mass direct action is the answer, or something along those lines'. Huw Lemmey, then working in the maintenance department at Goldsmiths, went to the protest with his brother, a couple of friends from Lima Zulu (an artist-run space in north London set up in 2008), and an anarchist group based at Goldsmiths called 'Autonomy and Solidarity', who had organised a 'militant worker-student black bloc'. Lemmey's flatmate had created a leaflet advocating non-accredited universities as a strategy in response to education cuts. 'Education is a Napster Moment', the leaflet read. Technology had made the education system unviable, 'like in the case of music rights'. Techno-utopian ideas like this were representative of a certain strand of student activism at the time.

Charlotte Grace headed towards Millbank with a bicycle-supported sound system that had been stored at a squat in Camberwell; she pushed the speakers into the middle of the square. Meanwhile Jamie Woodcock and a group of students from Manchester were confronted by demonstration stewards as they tried to make their way towards the commotion:

> When we got towards Millbank there were a bunch of NUS stewards and they said: 'you've gone the wrong way there is nothing happening here you should go back'. I remember saying to one of them: 'I can see something on fire. That's where we are going.' They said: 'you are not allowed to', and we just pushed past them.

The first lines of protesters entered the square outside Millbank Tower. Some entered the wrong part of the building, believing

1.    Crowds surround Millbank Tower while the world's press watch on (Ian Macdonald, 10/11/10)

it to be Conservative HQ. The section of the demonstration that had attempted to occupy BIS, James Butler included, also arrived at Millbank Tower. The spirit of the crowd was unlike anything many had experienced. Rather than a small minority, the whole crowd seemed to possess a 'spontaneous desire' for direct action. As James Butler recalled:

> It is a feeling that I have experienced only once since, in Parliament Square later in that period: that feeling of a huge spontaneous desire on the part of the crowd to actually join in with such a thing, a sense that something really was insufficient about the demonstration and how it had worked.

For Gupt Singh, 'there's something that you can't predict about it, either it works or it doesn't. And it was something where people, in their heads, in that moment, decided that this was the right thing to do, and that they were willing to give it a chance.' Kieran Sutton, a college student from Westminster Kingsway, remembers seeing graffiti on the floor: '"Don't fuck up our Future" – but spelt wrong. The "Future" was spelt "Futer". It's the first time I had been on a protest and felt "This is my generation".' Arnie Joahill describes the minutes before the ensuing mêlée:

> We turned our banner to face Millbank. The security didn't know what to do. From what happened then it was a blur. More people kept coming and the sound system followed under the arches of the building. The square kept filling up until it looked like the whole demo was there. What was so funny was that there were no police there: no TSG, no riot police. No one.

People started lighting bonfires of placards. We thought: 'this was it, we are staying'. At one point everyone was chanting in unison. There was a huge echo due to the shape of the building and it seemed like the windows were vibrating. I looked back and the sky looked red with anger. Everything looked tinged with red – flares, fires and anger.

Next thing you know, some anarchists turned up in black. A brick hit a window, coins started flying. One-penny coins are bouncing off the glass. Coins, cakes, placards and boots stomping on the window for an hour. At first there was only small cracks. There were still no police. It felt like we were invading. This is crazy, I thought, this is a government building. We will be on the news.

The police form in lines of two. They don't have riot gear on. They don't know what to do. They are totally overwhelmed. The window was being attacked from the front, the left and the side. I had a chest infection at the time and I was so crushed at one point I couldn't breathe. I felt like vomiting. There was smoke everywhere. I was tired. I was this coughing wreck.

There were about six or seven police inside. The lifts were closed and the ceiling lights were off. There was a doorway to the stairs and there was two or three security, trying to stop people climbing. Alarms are going off. The whole window had collapsed. People were spraying ACAB [All Cops Are Bastards] on the ceiling and Palestinian solidarity slogans were everywhere.

The police had not come prepared for this kind of protest. A report by Denis O'Connor, Her Majesty's Chief Inspector of Constabulary, in November 2009 had argued that officers

2.   Students take control of the building (Ian Macdonald, 10/11/10)

'risked losing public support by using aggressive tactics'
witnessed at the London G20 protests that year. O'Connor
criticised the police's outdated methods and insufficient regard
for human rights.[9] Although having a previous pedigree, it was
at the G20 protests that the police tactic of 'kettling' came to
national prominence. Such criticisms of police tactics, and the
death of innocent bystander Ian Tomlinson, had shaped police
strategy before Millbank.

Natalie Graham, an undergraduate from Leeds University
and activist with the climate group People & Planet, saw the

police overwhelmed by the protest. In the police line outside Millbank, she recalls, 'I remember seeing one of these officer's faces – he just had fear in his eyes, total fear. I remember that so vividly.' Not everyone felt sympathy for the police. Stuck inside the offices was Lady Warsi, the Conservative Party Chairman, along with much of the party staff. For Clare Solomon, it was the jeering from Conservative Party workers and heavy-handed policing that created a climate which pushed students to more direct action:

There were loads of Tory party workers who were kind of standing up on the balconies, goading and jeering at the students. The police themselves were also being quite provocative, pushing people when they didn't need to be pushed ... I think if I had to place blame somewhere, it'd be a combination of the Tories and police provoking the students.

While activists described a 'carnival' atmosphere at the base of the Tower, they were being filmed by a 'police helicopter which transmitted live images to a Lambeth control room a quarter of a mile away where a superintendent, the "Gold Commander", issued orders'.[10] For one of the students interviewed for this book, who wished to remain nameless, the police bore direct responsibility for the violence that occurred:

The cops tried to fight their way into Millbank – one line facing out and one facing in ... Where did the more militant stuff come from? It was because the cops came in and just went ballistic ... Initially people were smashing windows in order to get out of Millbank – it felt kind of scary being in there, being filmed by 24-hour TV whilst being hit by cops with batons … Occupying the ruling party's headquarters is quite significant, my Egyptian friend told me.

'Quite a few' of Natalie Graham's friends 'rushed into the building'. Her 'affinity group' was 'slightly more cautious', and although she 'was all for running in and getting to the top', her friends said 'nope, not going in there'.

For me, Millbank was about collective power. I had never felt more empowered in my life. When you're atomised and festering away in your room, thinking about things like climate change or capitalism, and suddenly you find yourself in a group of about four thousand people all as angry as you are, taking genuine action, it's seriously empowering.

Not all of Natalie's friends felt the same. Just as it was empowering for some, it also repulsed others. 'Some of my friends were absolutely shit-scared and pretty much never went to a protest again!', she recalled. 'One close friend at the time came away from it feeling like there's no hope for radical action.' For Clare Solomon, it was more of a 'carnival' than a riot.

It was literally like a carnival. Someone rocked in with a bicycle with sandwiches and snacks and those sort-of-things, giving them away. People had sound systems on wheels, people were dancing … People were cold so were burning placards. People dragged a sofa out from inside (the building); we were sitting on it watching the telly that was still going on inside the foyer. We were just sitting there in disbelief really … We were seeing a party, and the TV was reporting a riot … The atmosphere was a combination of the anger and the inspirational sort of feeling of hope that 'God, maybe we're able to do something here.'

Gordon Maloney, remembered that 'a lot of the people in the crowd didn't really know what was going on … but they weren't innocently dragged in'. By the time students had entered the building and started to climb the stairs, Conservative Party workers had barricaded themselves into the first and second floors, or had fled. Charlotte Grace recalled watching 'Tories flee from the fire escape' around the back of the building, where a group of party workers and secretaries had retreated behind a hedge, smoking cigarettes. There was a fistfight between a protester and a party worker, the latter coming off with a bloody nose as both clashed on the stairs.

There were Tories running down the stairwells with their files, with their ring binder folders … I have heard since that there were scuffles at the time in these stairwells when some people were trying to get up, and Tories were trying to get down … I'm not saying that they were carrying top secret documents … I know I saw them fleeing and I know I heard someone say, 'I just punched a Tory' … The foyer is intense and people are pulling over all the shelving units and the sofas. Then the lift goes 'ding!' and a TV comes out and people cheer and then it gets thrown through what I think was the last remaining pane of glass.

Inside the building Arnie Joahill witnessed anarchic scenes invisible to the crowds below:

The first and the second floor were locked. It was so funny that most of the Tory MPs locked themselves on those floors, scared for their lives or whatever. I remember going to the fourth and fifth floor, but not the roof. People were throwing around the computers, trashing the offices. People were spray-painting the walls, doing a complete makeover. Someone was even gluing internet sockets and electricity sockets and removing them so they couldn't work. Every single thing you could use in the office was being rendered effectively useless. There was a huge hole in one of the windows and I remember looking down through it at the thousands of people below.

Inside Millbank Tower youth from London, working-class and multi-ethnic, filmed music videos amid the disorder. On the fourth floor, Arnie Joahill saw 'people filming rap videos and stuff. It was crazy! These two guys from my school – one

3.    Protesters scale the roof (Ian Macdonald, 10/11/10)

rapping and the other filming – saying "fuck the government!"
… It felt like you were in some kind of rave but during the day.'

Arrests were made during and after the initial protest with
54 eventually made on the day itself, while ten people were
injured.[11] Nina Power describes how the 'scale of the arrests
and the behaviour of the police' during the protest meant there
'was a real need for campaigning on this issue in a very public
way'. The young people who ended up in jail were often very
similar to those from Arnie Joahill's school in west London,
who had left classes to come to the protests:

> My sixth form friends weren't heavily political … They
> were deprived people from very mixed areas. They didn't
> understand it from the 'left-right-centre' political spectrum.
> They understood the demonstration in a more angry and
> violent way. It was an anti-government and anti-police
> perspective: a street-politics understanding. No political
> organisation *really* connected with them.

There was a divide in how predominantly working-class
college students reacted to the violence in comparison to
those at universities. Jamie Woodcock explains the context of
the debates on the coach back to Manchester after the demonstration:

> For lots of the college students, violence from the police
> wasn't new to them. They lived in inner city Manchester,
> regularly harassed by cops and 'stopped and searched'.
> But for many of the university students, it was absolutely
> shocking … The cops at Millbank were lashing out almost

at random. There was no pushing, just straight out with the batons on the head.

The violence was not organised by an anarcho-militarist minority, but was driven by students with little or no political experience. The attempt to blame the protest on a 'militant plot' unwittingly enveloped Luke Cooper, a PhD student from Sussex. Cooper successfully sued the *Daily Mail* and the *Evening Standard*:

A journalist came up and asked me: 'who organised this?' I made the mistake of talking to him and gave him some very general soundbites. He twigged that I worked at a university, that I was a PhD student and an associate tutor. The journalist later found my staff profile on the Sussex University website. The story they wanted to pitch, which also implicated lecturers at Goldsmiths College, was something along the lines of: 'lecturers organise anarchy on the streets of London'. The press often likes to frame these things as militants behind the scenes pulling the strings, conspiring to commit violent disorder on Britain's streets ... The next day I was on the front page of the *Evening Standard* and the story was also picked up by the *Daily Mail* ... Looking back on it seems funny and ridiculous ... I went on to sue them in the High Court across five days in summer 2012 which was extremely stressful. I was awarded £60,000 in damages.

Two journalists from *The Times* didn't realise their mistake when they unwittingly interviewed 'Leila Khaled' (the name of an activist from the Popular Front for the Liberation of

Palestine, credited in the late 1960s as the first woman to hijack an airplane and banned from entering the United Kingdom), who they named as 'a student of the University of Essex' – printing her quotes in the newspaper the next day.[12]

The issue of 'violence' was a key theme of the movement, and the subject of incessant debates and vitriolic exchanges. Both Sally Hunt and Aaron Porter, Presidents of the UCU and NUS respectively, condemned the occupation of Millbank. Porter wrote in *The Sun* that it was 'despicable that a minority's violent actions hijacked a serious issue that 50,000 students came to protest'.[13] The discourse of 'extremist minorities' hijacking 'legitimate' protest, imposing themselves on 'normal' students, has a long history. This was a common refrain employed to explain and delegitimise the protests in the late 1960s. Geoffrey Martin, President of the NUS in 1968, condemned 'a minority of militants' and 'small extremist groups' for the sit-ins at universities throughout the country.[14] For *The Times*, writing of the 1968 protests, 'it is constantly repeated that the students who carry their intolerance to the borders of violence or anarchy are a very small proportion of the whole. That is doubtless true. But ... they have been able to impose their will on the majority, and in doing so are able to modify the character of their institutions.'[15] 'There was clearly a hard core that was militant and aggressive as well as those students who were disappointed [at the breaking of the pledge]', echoed Vince Cable.

In the aftermath of the demonstration, 'going into the NUS office was very difficult at times', recalled NUS Black Students' Officer Kanja Sesay. Aaron Porter felt that the individuals who had done criminal damage 'had harmed the campaign':

Many of those who went into Millbank were not students – many were but many were not. There was a risk that my comments might have upset students, but there was an even bigger risk of saying nothing. We would have been seen to be complicit with their actions. I think NUS as an organisation would have lost credibility, and, more importantly, we would have lost the respect of those we were trying to convince … The Liberal Democrats by this point were trying to find excuses not to engage with us … I accepted at the time that the demonstration was a double-edged sword. It unquestionably got us more press coverage than had it been a peaceful, respectful day … But that type of press coverage was unhelpful – it was about the tactics, not the issue … I regret the form of words I used … I should have been clearer to say that the actions were despicable, not the individuals … Justifiably that allowed a lot of people to feel very let down by me.

Some protesters saw the violence as a key asset for the movement. As Bob Crow, the late General Secretary of the RMT union, noted in a speech to the UCL occupation: 'Only when suffragettes broke windows did the world take notice.'[16] For Michael Chessum, a sabbatical officer at UCL student union, Millbank defined the student movement due to both the size of the demonstration and the direct action. 'The press line was: "look at what young people are forced to do to be heard", but really what we were thinking was "look at what people are *willing* to do".'

Certain actions by protestors, like property damage, were more easily justified than others. The dropping of the fire extinguisher from the roof of Millbank by Edward Woollard was one of the defining events of the demonstration.[17] For Clare Solomon, 'everybody straight away leapt to Edward Woollard's defence, as we all knew that it was a moment of madness, and he didn't think it through properly.' Charlotte Grace was standing only a meter away from the spot where it fell:

I look back at that moment now as one of the most horrific things that could have even happened to our generation. I get shivers when I think about it – not in terms of proximity, like 'it could have been me' or anything, but in terms of how that moment would then forever be seen, how politically that moment would have … been dead in the water.

A. described the feeling amongst those in the square:

After the fire extinguisher was dropped people started chanting 'stop dashing shit off the roof'. And that was, I guess, the low point of an otherwise spontaneous, in my eyes positive move, against what we believed at the time was a state which didn't care for working-class youngsters trying to make it out in the world ... The demonstration was the first moment where young people actually took control. There was a sense of genuine power amongst people on the ground. Engaging in an act which on the face of it didn't really do that much. But there was a sense of unity amongst everybody who was there.

Mark Bergfeld helped to organise an open letter, published in *The Guardian*, defending the Millbank protesters. Over 3,000 people signed the statement 'calling for unity to defeat the

Con-Dems' cuts' and standing 'with the protesters against vic-timization'. Billy Bragg, Naomi Klein, Paul Gilroy and several leading journalists and trade and student unionists signed. For Bergfeld, the unity statement was a key moment in 'how the leadership roles were reconfigured during the student movement'. Vicki Baars, NUS LGBT Officer, was one of the original instigators of the statement. Looking after younger students in her LGBT block at a pub in Victoria, she was able to draft a statement of support for the occupiers while the phones of other activists had run out of battery. Her first response was 'what is violence? Smashed windows of the Tory Party headquarters seem petty in comparison to the damage that party has done to people's lives.' Alexandra Chandran also remembered difficult arguments with students at Queen Mary University in the aftermath: 'We [activists] had lots of explaining to do.'

Not everyone was as willing to excuse the property damage or forgive the fire extinguisher incident. Hannah Sketchley, a first-year student at UCL not yet involved in activist politics, saw Millbank on the news: 'Everyone was like "isn't it awful" and I agreed. My politics developed fairly quickly over the subsequent few months.' Adam McGibbon also noted that the sabbatical officers at Queen's University Belfast, who had travelled all the way to London to go to the demonstration, were 'pretty angry about the Millbank Tower stuff – although now I think they would have different opinions'. However, this did not stop them from seeing the atmosphere as 'electric', and returning to Belfast with more energy to organise large events. Huw Lemmey recalled the scene at a pub in Victoria, filled with university lecturers who had been at the demonstration.

The older trade unionists discussed the images of Millbank relayed on the television news:

> The lecturers there were saying: 'oh they have ruined it'. People were looking to throw anything they could find on the big fires in the middle of Millbank. One lecturer made a comment, which at the time I didn't think was significant, but I now do. One of the shots on the screen was of students piling UCU trade-union placards on the fire and this guy was like 'they don't know what they're doing! I can't believe they've done that'. I can imagine if you are a UCU member you don't want to see your placards burnt on TV. But that comment felt symbolic in the months after. The students had no idea what these placards were; they just wanted to make a statement.

Coach journeys back from the protests were often just as important sites of memory for participants – and as politically formative – as the actual protests themselves. As Leeds University student Natalie Graham noted, one of the key images that stayed with her were 'the coach journeys back, when you're really tired and eating chocolate and weird food, and you're kind of sweaty'. Gordon Maloney remembers 'there was a real mixture of opinions on the coach going back' to Aberdeen. 'Lots of people didn't really know what had happened.' Jamie Woodcock remembers the importance of the 'five- or six-hour' coach journey for activists from Manchester, creating unity between university students and college students and a sense of common purpose. 'There was a real sense that you were going "as Manchester". That sense of a "we" became strong.'

For Joana Ramiro, originally from Portugal and the (unofficial) press officer for the National Campaign Against Fees and Cuts, it was 'the first time that I had heard the word "condone" in English'. Running between her flat (also media HQ for NCAFC) and the protest, she would draft and send press releases to a host of media contacts. 'The way that we, the students, were being portrayed as vandals and reckless needed to be challenged ... the response of "neither condone nor condemn" was almost spontaneous', she recalls. Nina Power had to 'run off during the middle of the protest' to write an article for *The Guardian*, in which she defended the actions of the students who were 'protesting for the future of others'. A key moment in the aftermath of the Millbank protest, which set the tone for the activist response to the protests, was Clare Solomon's appearance on the BBC's *Newsnight* programme, where she sought to defended the protesters in a debate with Jeremy Paxman and Aaron Porter. 'I was so nervous, it was the single most invigorating and draining day.'

As with other historic demonstrations – seething with emotive feeling, exploding as a touchstone to loathe or celebrate – the battle over Millbank's meaning was fierce. James Butler recounts one of the most salient pieces of political advice he was given at the time, on the way back from the demonstration:

A few friends and I ended up on the last train to Oxford – the 'slow service' back out of Paddington. I think I had a meeting with my supervisor the next day. I was with a couple of people, one who became a really close friend. They were saying things like: 'Look. Tomorrow and the day after a lot of people are going be saying: "it means this" or "it means that", or, "we should be in charge" or whatever – from the Socialist Workers Party to the Whitechapel Anarchist Group. Don't listen to them; it was you lot that did it, you know. You should allow yourself to go with it and *be changed by it* and don't let it be put in any of these boxes.' One of the best pieces of political advice I've ever been given.

Charlotte Grace was one of those who had never been to a protest before, and had nothing to compare her experiences with. Her life track, like for many others present, was radically shifted by the demonstration:

It's a bit surreal as it was my first major protest. That's the irony of it. The moment had no context for me, because nothing for me had happened before it. So whilst for others it was this huge, epic situation that they'd already been imagining or thinking about or at the least could *conceive* of, for me I'd just landed there. Right place, right time, right way sort of thing ... It was so profound: radicalising, unifying and formative. It was one of the most important experiences of my life.

Millbank set its own agenda. The demonstration gave Vicki Baars 'the hope that we had power beyond politely asking for things to change'. The pretence of respectable politics had been dropped and the spirit of direct action became increasingly normalised. New possibilities had been opened up. 'Until Millbank there was not a single conversation about us potentially stopping what the government was trying to do with university fees', argued Ashok Kumar. Aaron Bastani, active in the UCL occupation, saw Millbank lay down a radical dividing line: 'All of a sudden, if you're a liberal, then occupying the university seems pretty fluffy compared to smashing up the HQ of the ruling political party.'

Some demonstrations become historical landmarks. Others represent cultural and political touchstones that shape how we understand the waves of political generations. The Millbank demonstration was not the first nor will it be the last of these events. For British students of the 'long 1968' it was the Grosvenor Square demonstration against the Vietnam War; for Italian students it was the 'Battle of Valle Giulia' in March 1969 in Rome; for the French it was the 'Night of the Barricades' in May 1968. 'Standing on the roof of the Conservative Party headquarters, with my wheelchair right beside me, I thought 10 November had changed my life', activist Jody McIntyre wrote.[18] Such demonstrations take on mythic significance even for those who were not there. As Charlotte Grace noted, 'after Millbank, so many images and stories were reproduced in the media that it almost feels like I remember the stories more than the events themselves'. Demonstrations like these become reference points to celebrate, to reject, or by which to measure historical change – but never to forget. Over the 2010 student movement hangs the shadow of Millbank.

# CHAPTER THREE

# *Expectations*

'Nobody quite expected this ... We didn't expect suddenly to feel so powerful, and now – now we don't quite know what to do with it.'

Laurie Penny[1]

Few, it seems, expected Millbank. Neither the police, the National Union of Students, left-wing activists nor journalists foresaw the storm that developed on the 10th of November 2010. The lukewarm student campaign against 'top-up fees' only exacerbated the sensation of extraordinary discontinuity. 'Student demonstrations had no real history of disorder', remarked the Metropolitan Police Commissioner Sir Paul Stephenson.[2] 'We had dealt with student organisers before and I think we based it too much on history ... Obviously you realise the game has changed', he continued.[3] The chief architect of austerity, Conservative Chancellor George Osborne, claimed he wasn't surprised: 'This is exactly what we were expecting ... We are working to a five-year plan, a five-year parliament. It is going to be like this for the first few years. There will be pain but there will be gain at the end.'[4] The student revolt briefly challenged the complacency on the part of those in power.

The tuition fees battle further exacerbated the cleavage between young people and the political class. 'The age of party democracy has passed', political scientist Peter Mair wrote in 2013. 'Although the parties themselves remain, they have become so disconnected from the wider society, and pursue a form of competition that is so lacking in meaning, that they no longer seem capable of sustaining democracy in its present form.'⁵ This 'hollowing out' of democratic institutions had impacted both politicians and electorates. Those in government were accustomed to 'ruling the void'. As the voices of David Willetts and Vince Cable attest, the architects of the reforms were surprised by the strength of feeling elicited from hitherto demobilised young people. 'I think people [in the Conservative Party] were surprised' by the scale of the protests, Willetts noted. What those making the movement and those on its receiving end expected show two groups living in different worlds.

### Broken promises

In the mythology surrounding the student revolt, the Liberal Democrat 'betrayal' over tuition fees is foundational. All Liberal Democrat MPs had signed the NUS-organised 'pledge' to vote against any fee rise in the next parliamentary term. Aaron Porter, recently elected President of the NUS at the April 2010 conference, wanted to 'extract a public promise before the May 5th [2010] election'. 'We were worried about a potential consensus emerging between the three main parties in Westminster.'

The Liberal Democrats would pay a heavy price to enter government. Some leading figures in the party, like Vince

Cable, foresaw the problems posed by its tuition fees pledge. *The Guardian* reported leaked documents showing that the Liberal Democrats had decided to renege on the pledge two months before the general election.[6] Cable viewed signing up for the pledge campaign as a 'disastrous' idea:

My party colleagues realised that there was a train wreck coming ahead of us. In the run up to the 2010 election, we had a group of people who had been elected to our Federal Policy Committee for whom fighting tuition fees was their number one issue, and who were determined to have it in the manifesto. Nick Clegg, David Laws, Stephen Williams – most of our people – were adamantly opposed to it ... I was one of the few people that thought what the Labour government [which introduced tuition fees] did was quite sensible ... I could see no alternative than going down that road ... Quite apart from the difficulties around the policy, we knew there would probably be a Coalition government and we might be involved, and that there might be issues with public spending. Why get committed to something like that?

The [anti-tuition-fee] group in the party prevailed, despite our opposition. Then in a crucial decision that we are still paying for to this day, Nick Clegg decided the following day that we should be hung for a sheep as a lamb, and we should all sign up to the NUS pledge ... It was clearly very popular with our MPs in university seats – Manchester, Bristol, and Cambridge ... I was absolutely apoplectic about it and so was David Laws. The point was put to me, as Deputy Leader, that you can't publicly disagree with your leader in the run up to the general election. So we had to back him up and agree to support his pledge.

What had alienated our supporters was not the policy but the pledge. Once we couldn't honour the pledge we were on a hiding to nothing. The Labour Party had twice made pledges on tuition fees and twice broken them. We had rather assumed that we would pay a political price like they had – that it wouldn't be an epic issue like it turned out to be … At the time the consequences hadn't really been thought through.

Cable went from believing he could 'sidestep the problem' by not being involved in the decision-making, to being given the role of Business Secretary in the Coalition government. The Department for Business, Innovation and Skills oversaw the higher and further education sectors. 'As a result of a whole series of accidents and institutional rigidities, the Liberal Democrat Secretary of State was responsible for this policy.'

Greg Mulholland, Liberal Democrat MP for Leeds North West, believed that the Liberal Democrat manifesto policy and the tuition fees pledge were 'not the same thing' and had been 'deliberately conflated' by those who had never been reconciled to the policy. For Mulholland, not being able to deliver on the manifesto pledge to abolish tuition fees was 'not the same thing as then breaking the pledge' to vote against any increase in fees during the next parliamentary term. Not understanding the difference between the policy and the pledge was 'a disastrous mistake, and in many ways an inexcusable mistake' by the Liberal Democrat coalition negotiating team. Mulholland, who would lead the backbench rebellion against Cable, saw the pledge as a 'personal commitment from me with my name on it, like a cheque'. 'We then had this phony argument in the parliamentary party – very heated arguments as you can imagine', he remembered:

> The line was that the Coalition agreement had given us the right to abstain … But the pledge was for us to vote *against* any rise in fees, so abstaining would be breaking the pledge. More realistically, it was being fudged and conflated. It is upsetting to see the delusion of colleagues you know and work with, to see the delusions and dishonesty of some of the arguments to try and justify something that clearly is unjustifiable. The initial fault was with the negotiating team; the fault after was with those people in the department, BIS, and our team working on this policy – they failed to win the argument that we shouldn't move towards a system that involved increasing fees.

Tim Farron, the future party leader, also broke with his party leadership. 'Education should be available to all – not just those who can stomach the debt', he argued.[7] The rebels, however, were unable to coalesce around a common policy. 'I fear the alternative would be cuts in other areas like science or further education, which is why I'm hesitating to vote against', argued Martin Horwood – who was excused from voting while in Cancún for climate change talks.[8] David Willetts, Minister of State for Universities and Science, had 'made sure that Tory MPs and parliamentary candidates had not signed the pledge, and I had written out to all Tory candidates advising them not to sign'. Once in government he had argued for 'getting on with' the reforms. 'In my political experience these political decisions never get easier, and secondly the Treasury had set a programme of BIS departmental cuts and if we didn't do this then we would be doing far worse things.' Willetts was surprised by the turn of events:

We would have completely understood it if the Liberal Democrats turned around and said: 'we want nothing to do with this – we will all abstain'. It would have been tricky if they had all voted against. It would have been personally tricky for me, bringing in a policy with a Liberal Democrat colleague beside me – Vince sitting on his hands – but they could have done that. And the Tories were pretty surprised they didn't. But I think they got sucked into it and realised too late, and they split three ways ... We weren't doing this deliberately to damage the Liberal Democrats.

The 'betrayal' by the Liberal Democrats is central to the 'moral economy' of the student revolt.

*Policy and protest*

The student movement had been historically divided over tuition fees. In Northern Ireland, Adam McGibbon remembers 'there was disagreement with the unofficial campaign as to whether we should campaign for the right to free education or to cap tuition fees, and we ended up focusing on capping'. 'I kind of wanted free education too, but it was a case of what was realistic, and it was the right thing to do by students, and also something that really got through to the lawmakers ... I just didn't think that [free education] was on the table.' For Nina Power, the goals of the movement were clear: 'most people came from a "no-fees" position'. On the other hand,

Aaron Porter argued that the student movement needed to 'put forward a credible policy'. This entailed 'advocating some form of progressive contribution' – a 'graduate tax'. This position, Porter noted, had been passed with a large majority at the April 2010 NUS conference. 'Having a costed, credible position allowed us access to senior politicians.'

Porter describes how the 'early signs' in meetings with Vince Cable over the summer 'were that he wanted to resist any rise in tuition fees and actively look at a graduate tax':

I remember him saying at the conference that we would have to consider the viability of a £6,000 fee. I said we would potentially look at £6,000, but that we would have to find some democratic endorsement of it; either by a national student referenda or an emergency conference ... I couldn't on my own offer support for it, mainly because of the [2010] NUS conference position on the graduate tax, which I had to observe.

Cable also remembered the meeting with Porter and some of the NUS leadership at the Liberal Democrat conference:

As we neared the point where announcements about the policy needed to be made, it became clear that the students were going to react very badly. I had already sensed that there was a certain amount of posturing going on. I did meet the NUS Executive at the Liberal Democrat party conference. They said: 'if you can keep this down to £6,000 then we'll go through the motions of opposing it'. I remember meeting them at a coffee bar with the President and four or five of the Executive. The message I got was: 'we're not going to make a big deal out of the pledge itself, providing you keep this down'. I think the other thing that was beginning to happen was that the other NUS people understood what we were trying to do ... They knew that politically they had to make a fuss, but they weren't persuaded that it was something terrible. Whatever happened in the next two months, they realised that their membership was gagging for a fight, and you know what happened subsequently ... I don't think we did [expect the protests to be so large and violent].

Porter found it hard to read Cable's position:

It was never quite clear where he was coming from. I don't know, even today, whether Cable was uncomfortable with a marketised funding approach, or whether he was conscious of the Liberal Democrat promise, or whether he actually believed tuition fees were a bad thing. I don't know whether it was the lure of the policy or, more likely, that he was pushed by the fear that the graduate tax would bring down the Coalition within six months [that changed his position]. After the Liberal Democrat party conference Cable didn't meet me again.

The battle lines had been drawn between students and the government.

### The weight of history

The expectations of leading figures in Parliament and the NUS were shaped by parliamentary arithmetic and the constraining logic of austerity. Protesters and politicians worked on their decisions and strategy in isolation from one another.

Activists on the ground understood the emerging movement 'from below'. Many rationalised their experiences through historical analogy. Coming from Algeria, Malia Bouattia could filter and evaluate her experiences in the movement in Britain through a long history of anti-colonial struggle. '[You] constantly learn from those perspectives, but also see what works for them and what doesn't … I have a fresh perspective on the differences in tactics and where we need to strike. But further to that I don't see our struggle in isolation, which has been a problem for the UK student movement in the past.' Bouattia expected that the vote on tuition fees wouldn't pass due to the scale of the movement against it: 'I mean just because we've never seen, in my lifetime, such an eruption. [We've] never seen such an uprising. I was hopeful.'

No student revolt can avoid comparison with 1968. Many commentators made the analogy at the time.[9] Vince Cable experienced both, the second time in 'the eye of the storm':

> I have seen these movements come and go. I was a university lecturer in the late 1960s and early 1970s in the Vietnam era in Glasgow, so I'm not that unfamiliar with student protests … Since I was in the eye of the storm it was quite difficult to be detached about it [the comparison of 2010 to the 1960s]. But it did strike me.

The anti-war movement, more than 1968, was a key reference point. Aadam Muuse, a student at Sir John Cass Sixth Form College, remembered 'growing up for some of my life in Tower Hamlets, near East London mosque. It was the target of lots of racists. I would go to the demos against them and against Israel's occupation of Palestine. People from my community would organise to go to central London for these. Politics was always there.' It was through participating in the 2010 movement that he uncovered a hidden history of struggle at his school:

> I actually didn't know about the school walkouts against the Iraq War until I started to organise walkouts in my college in 2010. I bought a megaphone, stood outside the school, and would speak. Apparently some of the school kids could hear the talks, as they were on the other side of the building. That got me in trouble and I was threatened with suspension or possible expulsion … The head of sixth form called me in for a meeting. She talked of when school kids climbed the fence over the Iraq War, after a campaign of leafleting and megaphones. She was scared that what I was doing would allow that to happen again. She vividly remembered it.

Others, like Jamie Woodcock – a Masters student at Manchester University in 2010 – had participated as a school student in the demonstrations against the Iraq War in Oxford. He also took part in the 2009 occupations against Israel's Operation Cast Lead in Gaza and the 2009 G20 Summit Protests in London:

> The protests against the Iraq War were my first political experience. We staged walkouts from our school, we blocked roads. That was when I was 15 or 16 and it was my first experience of mass movements. I remember a teacher saying: 'You can't leave! You will be in so much trouble!' I said: 'Look behind you; the whole of the year group is

walking out – you can try and put us all in detention if you want.' Although [the anti-war movement] didn't win, when I went to university I had built this idea about it that it was a place that you could do activism.

Some school students, like Barnaby Raine, were primed to expect that demonstrating didn't always bring success. The largest demonstration in British history was unable to stop the Iraq War, so what chance did the students have?

Because I had been politicised by the anti-war movement, I didn't believe that demonstrations worked. There was no point at which I thought we were going to win; school students had organised fantastic walkouts in 2003, after all, and of course they failed to stop the war ... I never really believed that we would win, but just thought that it was imperative that we try.

For those deeply affected by the Iraq War, the feeling of betrayal amongst many young people who had first voted for the Liberal Democrats is hard to overestimate. The Liberal Democrats not only took a distinctive line on tuition fees, but had also opposed the Iraq War. This had major implications for how the movement developed. As Ben Beach explains:

Something that greatly impacted me was the Iraq War. After that, if you were young and left-leaning, you didn't like the Tories but you didn't like Labour either; meaning that 2010 led people towards the Liberal Democrats. The 'stab-in-the-back' of that betrayal meant the bottom just dropped out of politics. After that, everyone thought: 'well f- this then, we're going to have to do it ourselves'.

'From above' and 'from below', the preconceptions of politicians and students were shaped by historical precedent. Neither, however, expected the energy Millbank unleashed.

## Preparing for defeat

Although politically experienced activists in higher education were prepared for defeat early on, many school students were not. Will Searby, then a school student in Bath, recalled that he and many of his peers believed that the vote in Parliament would be defeated. The shrinking of the protests after the vote on December 9th, and the widespread demoralisation of school and further education students, attests to this. 'I think we expected to defeat the vote', said Will Searby. 'I wasn't alone in assuming that actually the vote was going to fall.' Some relatively new activists like Natalie Graham also believed that the fees wouldn't rise. But as the movement continued, and activist energies were sapped – especially through the problems involved in the Leeds occupation – her optimism started to fade. 'I really thought that the fees weren't going to go up. I think my optimism started to fall during the occupation. It was a space that had power being drained out of it, and it's exhausting. Also, the way that the demonstrations were represented in the media kind of gave me an insight into the forces that we're up against.' Alan Bailey, then NUS LGBT Officer, had high hopes for the transformative power of the movement. After Millbank, 'I thought: are we seeing something massive here? That it will continue to grow and spread ... Afterwards I came to realise that all this wasn't going to happen.' Michael Chessum explains how the strategy of the protest organisers didn't prepare participants for the consequences:

> We couldn't tell everyone that we thought we were going to lose. All we could give was a public message. There was no internal communication – the press line had by its nature to be dishonest ... We didn't do enough to prepare everyone else for that fact, especially those in further education, where demoralisation was worst.

The hopes of many new to politics, without previous experience of victory or defeat, made losing all the more painful and demoralising.

## Prefigurative pragmatism

Although formed to fight against fees and cuts, the movement developed into something more than a campaign. Protesting and occupying sometimes became ends in themselves. For many in the university occupations, thinking in terms of 'winning' and 'losing' was beside the point. Where the traditional politics of the elite had failed, students would build a new politics from where they were. For Aaron Bastani, 'a lot of people in the UCL occupation weren't thinking in those terms [of winning or losing] ... it was such a liminal space ... People genuinely weren't thinking instrumentally day to day. It was amazing really, you know how people say that capitalism is so deeply embedded in all of us, but in two weeks you can unlearn a lot of stuff.' For James Butler, based in Oxford, what could be achieved was a more important question than the vote over fees and the EMA – it was 'an opportunity to build a political culture that didn't exist, or, did, but in a sort of private sense':

> I always thought we were going to lose, which hardened me a bit. That stopped half-way through when we realised how strong the support was ... Where I was wrong was that I expected it to build quite a strong, wide political movement outside the confines of the student movement. It sort of happened for a little while, but not to the extent that I was expecting.

Kieran Sutton, from Tottenham, was in his final year of college at Westminster Kingsway in central London. For him the movement was about more than fees and cuts. Overcoming the cynicism of his friends, he learned life-long political lessons:

> Some of my friends were cynical at the time. 'Look what happened at Broadwater Farm in the 1980s', they said. 'Police killed someone, there were riots, but protest doesn't do anything' ... That said, I was very optimistic. I was very happy and stubborn. For the first time in my life I felt I was doing something positive with my life that wasn't just education.

For Clare Solomon, forming a new political generation was critical. 'Whilst we didn't stop the tuition fees being raised, we did inspire a whole generation of activists. I mean that's what actions and demonstrations are about anyways – not the immediate focus and demand, but giving people more confidence and insight into how the world works.' On the other hand, Joe Ryle – a student at Leeds University, previously active in the climate movement and who would go on to work for John McDonnell MP – saw his own approach as more 'pragmatic'. For Ryle, the goals of the movement were clear and needed no utopian projections:

> A lot of protest groups sometimes struggle to have a clear goal, but this time there was one: stop the rise in fees. That was my goal. I don't think I was thinking more deeply – some people were probably bounding it up in anti-capitalist messaging, but for me I have always worked more pragmatically: what can we actually achieve?

The tension between understanding the movement as a straightforward campaign to stop a government policy or as a moment in a longer process of politicisation structured how participants understood the revolt.

*Breaking the Coalition*

Potential weaknesses in the Coalition government played a key role in activists' expectations. While for Ronald Fraser's student generation of 1968 'there was never any serious doubt in the minds of British student leaders that revolution was not an immediate prospect in Britain',[10] some in the 2010 generation did envisage a new state of ungovernability. Explaining the failures of the British 1968, one student revolutionary noted that 'the British state, the whole political system in this country, had immensely more ideological authority amongst students than was the case on the Continent'.[11]

After the 'betrayal' by the Liberal Democrats and 30 years of political disengagement, the British state did not enjoy the same esteem in 2010. For Mark Bergfeld, the immediate expectation was to 'stop the fee hike', but because the 'vote was so central to the government's agenda', there was the possibility that the Coalition would 'break', forcing new elections. Sean Rillo-Raczka, then chair of Birkbeck Student Union, thought the Coalition could be broken: 'We did think it was possible: "they are wet liberals, they can be moved"'. Koshka Duff, postgraduate student, activist and feminist at Birkberk, thought it might have been possible to 'bring down the government by making the situation ungovernable':

> I was not that concerned with the tuition fee vote itself. It was not a massive shock to me that the vote went the other way. That was just how Parliament worked. I thought that the government was quite weak, and that divisions could be exacerbated. This meant creating a state of ungovernability. It wasn't that I thought 'this is definitely going to happen', but it was achievable, if, in response to repression, there was – I didn't use this word at the time – 'escalation'.

Jamie Woodcock remembers 'we said to people: "we are going to the demonstration to bring down the government"':

> We wanted to bring down the government and spark a wave of working-class struggle. Not insurmountably small aims … There were moments when you thought: 'this could be the moment of something much bigger' … It's much easier to look back in retrospect at these things.

Those who made the movement from below and those imposing the reforms from above viewed the revolt from totally different vantage points. Those on the receiving end of the protests changed their positions little, if at all. Why politicians took the positions they did had little, if anything, to do with the actions of the movement in the streets. Committed on an intellectual and political level to the necessity of austerity and the 'progressive' nature of their reforms, politicians were largely indifferent to the protest – even if they were 'surprised' by its size and anger. For those participants who experienced the student revolt from below, expectations varied and could change rapidly. They rationalised their experiences through a series of successive approximations of what was possible and necessary. For many students, the 'natural order' was put into question in 2010. Or, at least, it had the *potential* to be. In the end, their hopes were misplaced.

# CHAPTER FOUR

# *Street Fighting Youth*

John Berger described mass demonstrations as 'rehearsals for revolution'. Berger's 1968 essay, 'The Nature of Mass Demonstrations', suggested that 'any demonstration which lacks this element of rehearsal is better described as an officially encouraged public spectacle'.[1] Writing just after the infamous Grosvenor Square demonstration against the Vietnam War, Berger argued that mass demonstrations were spaces where those who feel outside political representation openly confront the state, the government and the forces of order. A mass demonstration is a '*created* event', he continues, 'which arbitrarily separates itself from ordinary life'.[2] Demonstrations raise consciousness of a common collective purpose and identity.

What emerged in 2010 was a 'created event' after this model – an explosion of creativity by those thought to be permanently alienated from the political system. After the Millbank demonstration on November 10th there seemed to be an irresistible momentum. Young people spontaneously organised themselves. Rosa Luxemburg described mass movements as a great wave or river, which 'flows now like a broad billow over the whole kingdom'; they divide 'into a gigantic network of narrow streams ... It bubbles forth from under the ground like a fresh spring and now is completely lost under the earth.'[3] So too hundreds of thousands of students were involved in demonstrations, occupations and walkouts across the country – a bubbling stream that seemed, for a time, unstoppable. This chapter tells the story of the transformation of a demonstration into a movement.

### 24th November 2010: London

At a National Campaign Against Fees and Cuts meeting before the Millbank demonstration, the call for a national school walkout was made for November 24th, to focus on the cuts to the EMA. Students now had a date on which to focus their energies. The day of the coming mass demonstrations and university occupations was named 'Day X' by the protest organisers. Subsequent demonstrations would be labelled Day $X^2$ (November 30th), and Day $X^3$ (December 9th).

On the 24th, the crowds started to form on Malet Street in central London from 11:30 a.m. Facing them were 800 police officers, twice as many as deployed at the Millbank demonstration. Eight Territorial Support Group (TSG) vans – housing the praetorian guard of Britain's riot police – lurk in the side streets. Protective armour bulged conspicuously out of their hi-vis jackets. The police were not keen for a repeat of the demonstration two weeks earlier. Entering Trafalgar Square from all sides, the stream of protesters congregated on the steps of Nelson's Column. Impetuous and eager, the marchers headed down Whitehall towards Parliament. Their way had been blocked by a thick row of police assembled at the entrance to Parliament Square, lined up behind an abandoned police van. Now penned in from all sides on the narrow confines of Whitehall, many students became restless.

Alex Moore, aged 17 and working as a day-labourer, recalled being brought to the protest with his friend 'C'. 'I was only told about the protest due to my friend C, who is now in prison … C wasn't very political or interested, but went because he wanted to have a bit of a laugh and enjoy the madness at the time.' Moore remembered the police van, parked just in front of the police kettle:

Coming down Whitehall people were smoking weed, drinking, dancing to music and being a nuisance … At every demonstration there are a demographic of people there who don't know what's going on and want to cause trouble … We come up to the police line at Parliament Square and a van that had been left … The van was from the late 1990s. It was a Y reg … twice the normal age of any police car I've seen, and probably one they wanted to get rid of … On being kettled the general feeling became panicked. You can't have that many people hanging around each other like that without problems arising. It was obviously a police tactic. It allowed the demonstration to start, but also to come to an abrupt end with the demonstrators looking like the aggressors.

Students were not engaging in conspiracy theories about the 'planted' police van, which was then vandalised. *The Times* reported police officers teasing students trying to make their way back to the demonstration by the Churchill War Rooms next to St James's Park. 'We are collecting for a new police people carrier. All donations welcome. I am not sure the last one we had was fully insured', an officer joked.[4] Footage emerged from a Sky News cameraman showing demonstrators 'milling

4. Students are kettled along Whitehall and surround the abandoned police van (Patrick O'Brien, 24/11/10)

around by a police van' posing no threat a full 12 minutes before the Met abandoned the van claiming their 'officers felt vulnerable'.[5] 'We figured the old van had been placed there to get good pictures of youths trying to set it alight and putting graffiti on it', recalled Alexandra Chandran. The police van was vandalised and its contents raided. A police helmet and a bag of crisps were distributed amongst the crowd.[6] Schoolgirls obstructed the marauders by linking hands around the vehicle, much to the praise of *Guardian* journalists.[7]

With the vandalism of the police van as a pretext, the kettle tightened and split the demonstration in two. Alexandra Chandran witnessed a 'shared panic' as the police swooped across Whitehall and attempted to lock in a mass of demonstrators. She felt very 'apprehensive' due to her experience of the crush at Millbank. Civil servants and government officials watched from their windows as the students were slowly pacified in the confined space, many taking photos as mementos. Without recourse to an exit, toilet facilities or food and water, students in school uniform burned their exercise books for warmth as the temperatures began to drop. Unlike at Millbank, the police had come prepared for retribution. 'The game has changed', Sir Paul Stephenson said.[8] The Metropolitan police claimed the tactics were necessary to 'make sure the violence didn't spread across the London streets'.[9] Kieran Sutton remembers the crush as protestors tried to exit via the arches that separate Whitehall from Horse Guard's Parade:

> People were saying things like 'let me out my mum's at home expecting me'. Young Somali girls on their first ever demo were saying: 'I am going to get in serious trouble if I don't go home right now.' The mood changed and people went 'f- it', this is what it's about – we will take it to you. People started grouping around each other like 'what are we going to do?'

As the battle lines between protesters and police formed, John McDonnell MP arrived from Parliament to show solidarity with the students. Both Kieran Sutton and Ed Maltby remember the Labour MP participating in a showdown with the police. Maltby describes the impromptu address given by the future Shadow Chancellor:

> Those who were outside the kettle – roughly equal in numbers to the people who were inside – were being pushed up Whitehall towards Trafalgar Square. And as we went up that way we saw squadrons of police horses coming down

Whitehall, spread out across the road. We all knew that the thing to do with police horses – we'd read this somewhere on the internet – is to sit down in front of them, because they don't like walking over people, apparently. So we all sat down in front of the police horses. On his way walking down to Parliament or to Portcullis House … John McDonnell is walking down the street. And somebody yells at him: 'Hey, John, what are you doing? Come and make a speech, John.' John McDonnell came over to where we were, sat there right in the middle of a row of people, and linked his elbows with people around him. Someone passed him a megaphone and he started testifying. That's our current Shadow Chancellor.

According to Kieran Sutton, this intervention by McDonnell avoided a nasty confrontation with the police:

The police had seemed to lose control of the situation. As we were sitting in rows in front of a police line, two or three riot vans turned up with officers all in riot gear … The police were going: 'right you are going to get it'. But then John McDonnell comes over and sat next to us and the police were like: 'whoa – that's an MP'. I saw the officer talking to the sergeant, and then they turned tail. They took their riot gear off and went off. If John McDonnell reads this – he's a sick guy!

As the sun set and the temperatures plummeted, bins were set alight, bus shelters were used for impromptu raves, and fences from ongoing building works were used as wedges to break through the police lines. Students cheered when one hooded demonstrator daubed the word *Revolution* in red paint on the

5.    Students use a bus shelter for a makeshift rave (Patrick O'Brien, 24/11/10).

white wall of Whitehall. The first horse charge of the protests occurred just south of Trafalgar Square as police tried to break up the group of a thousand protesters outside the kettle. The charge was denied by the police until footage emerged on a protester's phone the day after which showed a pregnant woman in distress during the incident.[10] Eleven witnesses, in addition to journalists, claimed they were charged by horses at around 7 p.m.[11] Alexandra Chandran describes emerging from the kettle after 10 p.m.

> When we finally got out a police officer said to us with a smile on his face: 'oh, are you a bit cold? A bit tired? Just jog on the spot a bit.' My friend burst into tears. The discrepancy from what she had experienced in the kettle and the attitude of the policeman – as if it had been nothing at all … They were really saying: 'if you want to keep protesting, this is

how you will be treated'. After that moment I started learning more about police violence and deaths in police custody – after seeing the police in practice. That experience got me interested in pursuing law.

One student, S.G., who wished to remain anonymous, had experienced the police as a constant presence in their life. The movement of 2010 'only solidified' what they already thought:

> I had my opinions of the police already. I have always disliked them. We grew up in a culture where ethnic minorities in certain areas of London would be victimised by the police. They would harass you walking down the street, with constant 'stop and search' … That sentiment was reciprocated by me. 2010 only solidified what I already believed: the police are bastards.

6. With school in the morning, the long wait to leave the kettle begins (Patrick O'Brien, 24/11/10)

As university students were busy occupying their universities, the role of London school students in driving on the demonstrations was critical. Ed Maltby noted the changing demographics of the London protests, as the 'immense movement around the EMA cut, by mainly working-class, ethnically diverse, school and further education students' transformed the demonstrations. One of the most successful college walkouts in London occurred at Westminster Kingsway College. Kanja Sesay remembers the NUS Black Students' Campaign saw the college as a key organising target. Students organised themselves on the inside while older university-level students offered support outside. Kieran Sutton helped organise the walkout on the 24th:

> We got our banner out, I got a megaphone somehow, and we took the street down Gray's Inn Road to Malet Street with 60 to 100 sixth formers … The campus has maybe 500 people, so one in five came out … We were all just egging each other on – like 'should we go into the road … yes let's do it'. We were pushing each other on. I remember vividly going along that road, chanting. I was with people with whom I had never thought I would mix, doing something I cared about … It felt like it really shook the college building … everybody knew about it and everybody was talking about it. There was an electric atmosphere.

For Ashok Kumar, one of the most vivid memories of the movement was the division between the 'leaders of the movement – white, university educated, Russell Group institutions – versus the people actually coming in the streets'. Very rarely did these students find a voice in popular coverage of the protests. An exception was an interview with a masked and hooded protester for a video recorded for *The Guardian*. 'We had to make a statement', the student says, surrounded by his friends steps away from the police van. 'We're not having it. This is London students talking.'[12] Huw Lemmey saw one of the greatest strengths of the movement as the 'tens of thousands of inner city youth' who brought their 'energy … their own political consciousness based on what had happened in their lives; their hatred of any politician; their unwillingness to take orders; their ability to fight cops'.

After 10 p.m. the kettle was slowly emptied and the students could return home. Many had to be back at school the next day. Some had to go without their exercise books, burnt for warmth in the kettle the night before.

*24th November 2010: across the country*

The demonstration on the 24th November played host to many school walkouts across the country. As well as at several colleges in London, there were walkouts and demonstrations in Cambridge, Bristol, Leeds, Newcastle, Sheffield, Winchester, Hull, Bury, Milton Keynes, Colchester, Bournemouth and Halifax. James Butler, a PhD student at Oxford University, had also been in secret talks with school students at the local Cherwell School about a planned walkout. 'A couple of school students had been coming to our Oxford Education Campaign meetings [which organised the movement in Oxford], and told us that a lot of their students wanted to walkout.' A group of activists from the university 'went up to the school with this sound system in a shopping trolley, and these kids came out'.

There was also a very strong school students' movement in Manchester during 2010. Although largely self-organised, university students made a priority of agitating at local schools. A new and unitary political constituency was being formed in those weeks, as the divide between age groups started to break down. Jamie Woodcock remembers trying to urge school students to walk out with leaflets, only to find they had organised themselves:

> I used to live next to a college where I lived in Manchester and I would go with friends and 1,000 leaflets, giving them to the college students when they came out ... They said: 'Yes, we are going to organise a walkout' and we said 'alright...'. Then 400 came out, with students climbing over the fences ... Half of those we took to the demos on the buses were school students. We told the student union they were university students, as they wouldn't have been able to afford the bus otherwise. We would talk with them about tactics and what we had learnt from other movements.

Ed McNally took part in a walkout from Chorton High School in Manchester. 'I had watched the Millbank demo on the TV, though none of us knew about it as school students. We weren't in any networks to be aware of it.' The protest 'organised almost exclusively through Facebook' involved about '30 to 40 of mainly year 10 and year 11 students taking the number 86 bus to Manchester city centre for the day of action on the 24th November'.

> The staff at school had caught wind of our plan, and tried to make sure we needed signed notes from parents. Those

who didn't jumped over the gates. There was an age divide. For many of the very young students (those around 13 years old) it was about just bunking school and running away from the police. The Year 11s were more conscious and were very angry over the cuts to EMA. We all felt the unfairness of it all. As we walked out of the school grounds one of the teachers was very scathing. 'They don't know what it's all about – they don't understand politics', they said. Lots of the teachers the next day were very condescending. The walkouts were really unprecedented – with possibly only the walkouts over the Iraq War in recent memory – so maybe they were just taken aback. The movement had all but fizzled out by the 30th of November at my school, when much fewer attended.

Teachers were caught between their legally defined pastoral role and the self-activated student body. The head of the sixth form at Aadam Muuse's school proposed 'a day of letter writing to our MP as an alternative' to protesting. 'It was confusing as on the one hand she said she was proud of me, but also said I was using the wrong tactics.' Head teachers in Liverpool exhibited similar attitudes to the protests as those in Ed McNally's and Aadam Muuse's schools, believing protesting shouldn't affect students' school responsibilities. The head teacher of St Margaret's Church of England Technology and Language College, Dr David Dennison, said any protests by his students should be 'done in a manner that would not be detrimental to their present courses'.[13] Brigid Halligan, head teacher of Sefton Park Secondary Modern, worried that young children would think this protesting is a really good idea 'without really understanding what they are doing it for'.[14] This response was not shared by all teachers, some who actively encouraged their students and situated their protests in a longer tradition of radicalism. Sixth formers in Bath from the Ralph Allen School took to the streets 'with support of their head teacher Libby Lee'.[15] Hundreds of pupils from Unity College in Burnley staged a walkout and petitioned the local MP, Gordon Birthwistle. Head teacher Sally Cryer called the students' action 'spirited'.[16] 'I don't agree with protests and missing lessons', she said, 'but the students are passionate about their learning.'[17] A. remembered that his teachers were 'very pro':

> In fact, I don't remember getting in trouble despite actually being on a very tight leash with my history teacher. I remember missing a lesson and on the day after he asked me what happened. I remember me filling him in and then him trying to give me a synopsis of how it paralleled with the Peterloo Massacre.

Walkouts didn't just occur in major cities. The scale of the movement can be seen in the mass walkouts that occurred in towns across England, many of which had not seen such protests in decades. Will D. describes organising a walkout from his school in the small market town of Buckingham:

> My friend and I decided we should do something, and we settled on a walkout. We actually asked the headmaster if we could do one. He said: 'I really like that you are getting politically engaged. However, we can't give you time off lessons but we can give you a megaphone to give speeches in the school bus bays.' ... We thought the action would

be more transgressive if we actually missed lessons. We organised the demonstration through a fake Facebook account for the stray cat that walked through school called Humphrey. 'Humphrey Cat' was Facebook friends with everyone in the school, and I had been given the account details by someone in the year above at school ... Everyone at school thought that was hilarious. The novelty cat Facebook account is suddenly saying 'f- it guys, let's bunk school'. We had no plan on where to go or anything. It got to the day and we were thinking: 'are we going to go through with this?' I had come out of the morning break between lessons and saw this huge column of 250 to 400 people (mostly from the sixth form but also from the lower years) leaving school with my friend Alex leading them into town. Buckingham just happened to be the place where Nigel Farage, then UKIP leader, had an office. He came out as we arrived and we shouted: 'fuck you'. He quickly got into the car. Unfortunately, it was only a minority of kids who felt very dearly about the rise in fees and cuts to EMA. The rest were nihilists. There were a bunch of kids that turned up with signs that said: 'I'm not here for the politics, I'm just here for a party.' The Conservatives had won our mock school elections in May, and UKIP had come second ... We walked around shouting at nothing in particular. There is no establishment to confront in Buckingham. There is no Millbank. Then people started drifting off after a couple of hours, maybe back to lessons in the afternoon. A couple of days later a group of us were assembled and brought out of class and disciplined in a big assembly. I never ended up going to my detention.

Some schools and colleges mobilised more than others. 'Not that many ended up going' at Aadam Muuse's college in Tower Hamlets. However, those that did walkout had connections to previous waves of protests which the movement brought to light. 'There were about 10 of us ... I was confused at seeing some friends from school there, but it turned out that they had a long history of organising and had parents involved in anti-fascist politics.' A college student from Sheffield remembered a walkout of 63 people from his school commandeering a bus to go to a protest in the city centre for the 3,000-strong demonstration.[18] Like in Tower Hamlets, students brought with them symbols of other struggles. 'The crowd was very mixed. There were a lot of Somali kids there and poor white working-class students as well ... One of the students had brought a Palestinian flag.'[19] The movement activated hidden protest traditions, as students sought to make links between different struggles.

November 24th was one of the largest student mobilisations in British history, with thousands organising walkouts, demonstrations and occupations across the country. As students were kettled in London, others had taken control of university buildings or climbed over the fences of their schools. Students had to confront not just the government, but also their teachers and school administrators, intent on preventing walkouts. With little or no organisation, political experience, or outside agitation, British students showed they could build a mass movement few had believed possible.

## 30th November 2010

November 30th saw the third of the four major demonstrations held during the British student revolt. The demonstrations were largely self-organised, taking place in Brighton, Birmingham, Bristol, Manchester, Newcastle, Oxford and London, among other places. MPs couldn't understand the new tactics the students were developing: 'one of the features of the demonstrations that have taken place so far is that although the police have taken great pains to communicate with the organisers, sadly the organisers have then not appeared to be able to maintain the demonstration as originally suggested', one Tory MP lamented.[20] The protests were smaller on the 30th than on the 24th, but they were still substantial in both their size and radicalism. The students wanted to avoid the kettling which had marred the protests on the week before. The day played host to many messy and unruly protests.

As on the 24th, it was school and college students who took the lead. In Oxford, sixth formers and university students attempted to storm Oxford County Hall. Two students reached the roof, to the elation of the crowd. Talking to the local newspaper, Dan Bowen, aged 17 and from Cherwell School, acknowledged the example set by the university students: 'We saw what the university students did last week at the Radcliffe Camera [which they had occupied], and we want to do the same.'[21] Looking down from his office was Keith Mitchell, the leader of Oxfordshire County Council. He tweeted: 'County Hall invaded by an ugly, badly-dressed student rabble. God help us if this is our future.'[22]

Exeter city centre hosted to a 300-person demonstration. Students at the local ISCA College of Media Arts snubbed their head teacher Mandi Street, who had forbidden them 'to leave school premises, posted staff on exits, and had alerted the police.'[23] 'Although we cannot physically prevent children leaving the school, we have a duty to make sure they are safe.

That is why we informed parents and the police', she said. As in the week before, many teachers chose to act as disciplining agents to shut down the movement.

The protest on the 30th in London would become infamous as the 'cat and mouse demonstration'. Protesters were chased around London for hours by the police in sleet and snow. The police were unable to control the 4,000 assembled demonstrators after they split into smaller groups. Demonstrators congregated in Trafalgar Square from noon. Metal barriers and lines of police officers could be seen stretched along Whitehall, waiting for the marchers. Some impromptu stewarding marshalled the crowd away from Whitehall and down The Mall. 'We'd gone on a jog for miles and miles and miles that had taken us from Trafalgar Square to Victoria, Oxford Circus, with some people even making it as far as St Paul's Cathedral and Farringdon', Ed Maltby remembered. Huw Lemmey calculated that he and his friends 'had walked around 10 miles, running in and out of buses; these fat coppers trying to keep up but they just couldn't. It was really fun and chaotic.' Arriving back at Trafalgar Square, Alexandra Chandran remembers the police cracking down on the assembled protesters: 'the police were very pissed off that we had given them a run around central London, and wanted to get their own back'. The demonstration was to end yet again in a kettle. A total of 153 would be arrested. School students as young as 15 were kept in the freezing cold. The police charged the remaining protesters with batons. As the kettle was eventually cleared, graffiti left on Nelson's Column remained – 'No 2 Cuts' it said.

The demonstrations on the 30th November showed a maturing of the movement. Students quickly adapted to the new police tactic of kettling by maintaining mobility and speed. The numbers on the demonstrations had declined since the peak of the previous week, yet the radicalism remained. As the movement entered December, activists across the country focused their mobilisation on what was to become one of the most violent protests in modern British history.

*9th December 2010*

Parliament Square, 9th of December 2010. Not since the poll tax protest on the 30th of March 1990 had London experienced such a fierce confrontation. The Coalition government had brought forward the date of the vote in Parliament, under increasing pressure from the growing movement. On a bitterly cold day in December, with the Christmas holidays soon approaching, protesters and police prepared for a final confrontation. Assembling from 11.45, crowds of students prepared for the demonstration to set off from ULU in Bloomsbury. The parliamentary debate on fees started at 1 p.m. with a speech by Vince Cable, just as the students began to march down Malet Street.

Occupiers at UCL had been working hard in preparation, eliciting advice from many quarters. According to Ben Beach, the late Bob Crow – then General Secretary of the RMT trade union – came to the UCL occupation and 'warned us about our phones being tapped and gave us counter-surveillance tips'. James Butler describes preparing for the demonstration:

> I met some people at the UCL occupation, and prepared for the demo at Parliament Square with a series of meetings; 'know your rights' sessions, 'what to wear', 'what to do when police are police'. We'd come in colourful clothes, to change

into black or whatever, to avoid police surveillance. We were becoming quite – paranoid is the wrong word here – aware of how surveillance worked.

Student movements have historically been highly receptive to tactics tested by overseas movements. The tactics of Japanese students, organised in the Zengakuren federation, influenced students around the world in the 1960s. Equipped with helmets, shields and lances, they engaged in pitched battles against the police and formed 'snake marches' around Japan's Parliament. On learning how students in Warsaw responded to an official Communist Party speaker, Manchester University students in the 1970s chose not to heckle a Tory speaker, instead greeting him with applause and ironic over-enthusiasm at every sentence.[24]

Protest tactics also crossed borders in 2010. Concurrent movements in Greece and Italy offered new tactics and the sense of international revolt. The Italian student protests descended into 'urban warfare' as burning barricades were erected and demonstrators marched on Parliament.[25] The unexpected scale of the violence drew comparisons with the social unrest that swept across Italy in the late 1970s, forcing a national debate. At the London protest, Matt Cole was part of the famous 'book bloc', copied from the Italian students. Made of Plexiglas, foam rubber, cardboard and make-shift straps for arms, these book-shields were first tested by students from La Sapienza University in Rome on the 23rd of November 2010. On December 9th, the London march reached Parliament Square at around 1.30 p.m., halting at a police line. The assembled tomes and their carriers made their way to the front. Pushing began as a barrage of police truncheons rained down on *Endgame by* Samuel Beckett, *Negative Dialectics* by Theodor Adorno, *Society of the Spectacle* by Guy Debord, *Just William* by Richmal Crompton and *Specters of Marx* by Jacques Derrida. 'All the books went to the front of the march and as we got to Parliament they pushed through the police. Once behind the cops, they couldn't do anything. People then poured into the square', Cole remembers. 'My book was *Specters of Marx* by Derrida. There is a great photo of a police baton coming right down on the book, which appeared in the exhibition Disobedient Objects at the Victoria and Albert Museum in 2014.'

As the protesters streamed into Parliament Square a group of five activists were forcibly ejected from the public gallery in the House of Commons at 1.45 p.m., for shouting slogans during the debate. Outside, pitched battles commenced. Both the police and a large section of the protesters were ready for violent confrontation. Gupt Singh remembers protesters tearing down the fences set up around the grass on the square: 'It was a mad day.'

Clashes erupted at the barriers set up by the police to defend Parliament. Protesters surged forward, passing torn-down fences over the assembled heads to rain down on the police. At 3.45 p.m. the kettle began. Gordon Maloney recalls those on the front line rattling the gates, with the police hitting the hands of protesters. 'I remember seeing a sergeant walking down the line of police saying "aim for their faces". You could see they stopped swinging for arms and started hitting jaws.' 'People had passed the stage of being afraid of the police and what might happen', remembered Kieran Sutton. 'People were giving back what they got. They weren't scared anymore. It was unifying – people from different backgrounds, postcodes and races, coming together.'

By now caged inside the confines of Parliament Square by a solid kettle at each exit, some protesters tried to make a break through to Victoria station. Paint grenades made of light bulbs filled with acrylic paint were thrown, flashbangs set off. In scenes reminiscent of the 1984 miners' strike or the poll tax riots, unarmed teenagers faced a line of mounted police ready to charge. 'The officers' visors resemble those of Oliver Cromwell's cavalry', a journalist remarked.[26] Gordon Maloney witnessed it first-hand:

> I remember the first charge of horses. Nobody could believe what was happening. It was something that you hear about

7.    In scenes reminiscent of the poll tax riots, mounted police charge the students (Patrick O'Brien, 09/12/10)

and see in old movies … Someone who I didn't know but was with got hit on the head with a truncheon. I saw him a minute later; he was dizzy, couldn't stand up straight, and as I pulled him back from the crowd he collapsed in my arms. I was calling to these two police medics on the other side of the railing. They laughed at us and walked off. Later other medics took him away on a stretcher. I don't know what happened to him.

As the battle raged outside Parliament, the debate continued inside. At 4.10 p.m., Jeremy Corbyn MP condemned the actions of the police: 'Surely we want to send out the message that we welcome students to London', he said. If this bill is passed, Corbyn continued, 'we are destroying the opportunities, hopes and life chances of a whole generation … I signed a pledge not to vote for a fees increase, I voted against the fees increase in 2004 and I voted against the introduction of fees in 1998.'[27]

As students battled it out with the police and MPs finished the debate, the NUS was hosting a poorly attended 'glow-stick vigil for education' nearby on the Strand. The NUS NEC had voted on December 6th not to join forces with the national demonstration planned by the NCAFC and EAN.[28] Assembled complete with a 'disco bus', the NUS leadership had 'completely missed the mood of the youngsters', noted Clare Solomon. The 'rally' on the Strand was part of a 'dual strategy', remembered Aaron Porter. On the one hand, there was the demonstration outside and on the other there was a lobbying effort inside:

We had mixed messages from student unions. Some were saying: 'don't waste your time – it won't change anyone's mind'. This was largely my opinion. We therefore hired a committee room in the House of Commons, which allowed us to go out and lobby MPs. And I gather we were successful in convincing a few additional Liberal Democrats on the day. The suggestion for that demonstration, on the other hand, came from UCU.

If the NUS missed the mood of the youngsters, so too did some of the traditional far-left groups. Craig Gent saw this first-hand:

I remember to the one side of me seeing one socialist group, arms around each other, all singing the *Internationale* ... and on the other side was this group of young people of colour, probably further education students, arms around each other going: 'Let's go fucking mental, let's go fucking mental, la la la la hey!' And to me that sums up the disconnect between the Trot groups and 'the class', you know.

As the afternoon progressed, there was a lull in clashes on the edges of the kettle. Protesters danced around portable sound systems and argued about politics with their friends. Next to small bonfires of placards and left-wing newspapers, impromptu democratic experiments emerged, with groups discussing 'the way forward' for the movement. 'They spoke of everything they had experienced: police brutality, racism, dead-end jobs they would have for the rest of their lives', remembered Gupt Singh.

One of the movement's most poignant moments came in an interview by Paul Mason, then a journalist for the BBC's *Newsnight*, with a young man whose face was covered in a mask. He speaks directly to the camera: 'We are from the slums of London. EMA is the only thing that's keeping us in college. What's keeping us from doing drug deals on the street? Nothing.'[29] The interviewee was as far from the stereotype of Russell Group students and 'Lacan-reading hipsters' as one could get.[30] For Aadam Muuse, 'that message really struck a chord in my area, Tower Hamlets'. 'The only way out of that condition of extreme powerlessness was to use an education to make opportunities for after – to provide for our families by getting a better paid job, or even the temporary respite from those conditions by going away to university', Muuse continued. For Gupt Singh, 'those few words say more than any politician could to describe what was happening in those days':

> We're talking about kids, the majority of which were under the age of twenty, and many of whom were kids from London, you know, working-class kids, who were just … for them, this was like … I don't think they saw it more than as a chance to get their own back. Symbolically, if nothing else. And for me that really spoke volumes about what the content of the demonstration was politically. New, young and angry. Really, really, angry.

What made the December 9th demonstration unprecedented was not just the violence, but the diversity of those present. The demonstration played host to a brief yet powerful new social amalgam: the 'graduate without a future' uniting with the *banlieue* youth from the 'slums of London'. Mark Fisher, present on the demonstration, chided Paul Mason: 'Paul Mason dismissed the idea that the demo was exclusively populated by "Lacan-reading hipsters from Spitalfields" – but of course (we) Lacan-reading hipsters were also there, *alongside* the '*banlieue-style* youth from Croydon, Peckham, the council estates of Islington'. In other words, this brought together working class culture and bohemia.'[31] Nowhere was this amalgam more pronounced than in the changing music played on the portable sound systems carried to the demonstration by 'hardened protesters'. Shereen Prasad, having left school to attend the demonstration, remembers being originally confused by the music of the older protesters – 'I think it was Dub.'

> At the time I was like: 'what the f- is this shit'. My brother was like: 'this is what people listen to mostly at university age'. I was like: 'this isn't my crowd'. And I turned to some other school kids that I'd met on the demo and we were like: 'what the f- are these people listening too?' 'I don't know', they said ... There was a counter action against the Dubstep as people thought Dubstep was so bad.

The portable speakers were accosted by teenagers vying for the speaker-jack to plug in their iPod or Blackberry. Tightly packed dancefloors formed around the speakers. A video taken at the demonstration shows two young men dancing topless in the sub-zero temperatures to Lethal Bizzle's song 'Pow!'[32] Older generations of musicians have lamented the death of 'protest music'.[33] Yet they forget that the 2010 generation had their own. Grime, a music genre born in east London in the early 2000s, encompasses rapid breakbeats over which an MC 'spits' lyrics, usually concerning the gritty urban life of working-class youth. Grime's political urgency isn't 'about the content, it's

8. A grime rave continues despite sub-zero temperatures as protesters dance to Lethal Bizzle's track 'Pow! (Forward)' (Patrick O'Brien, 09/12/10)

about the energy and aura', argued Tempa T – a Grime MC whose tracks featured heavily on the protests.[34] The genre was a musical challenge to authority, shaped by the same physicality and anger which defined the student revolt's spirit.

Back in Parliament Square, Big Ben strikes six as night falls. The news spreads rapidly that the vote has been passed by 323 votes to 302. Tuition fees would be raised after all. The movement had failed to shift the government's position. Attempts to delay the vote by Liberal Democrat MP Greg Mulholland had failed.[35] MPs and Peers slipped silently through the police cordons, unnoticed by protesters. A. recalls the sense of desolation felt amongst his friends:

> I wholeheartedly believed that it would not go through. And
> I think that was a sentiment shared by every single person I

went there with and every single person that we confronted and spoke to. And the feeling was ... It's difficult to explain in words. Lost. There was a moment where everybody just felt lost for a few minutes. When word got out it spread like wildfire.

After the news had spread through the crowd, many students tried to go home. They found their route blocked by lines of police at every exit. Theresa May, then Home Secretary, claimed in Parliament days after that although a 'cordon was placed around Parliament Square ... throughout [the protest] those who remained peaceful and wished to leave via Whitehall were able to do so'. Those that chose to stay 'committed acts of violent disorder'.[36] These comments are contested by all those interviewed. Gordon Maloney was unable to exit the square for hours: 'every policeman you spoke too said you could leave if you went to the other section of the kettle, but when you got there it was also closed. This happened again and again. It became obvious that it was completely shut.' An hour after the news of the vote had broken, it became clear that the police had caged the remaining protesters in the sub-zero temperatures. The demonstration turned violent. One participant, who wished to be named 'Anonymous', 'had never seen that level of violence before':

There was a lot of fighting in the evening on Whitehall. These lads had found these huge scaffolding poles. They were really trying to kill the cops. I had never seen that level of real violence before. And the cops had their long shields and were fighting back. When scaffolding poles leave your hands it has this strength and power. Four protesters would throw it at close distance and just smash the shit out of them [the police]. The police sent in a snatch squad but got split up. These two cops were trapped, they drew batons, people threw stuff, and then another snatch squad came and rescued them. People were smashing the windows of the Treasury and shouting: 'we want our money back!' I was very impressed at the architecture of buildings. They were totally bombproofed...

The only thing that was unpleasant was when my friend was mugged in the kettle in Parliament Square for his Blackberry. I stepped in and caught his hand and pulled it back. My friend ran and a 16-year-old kid pulled a knife on me. Then his mate pushed him on the chest and said: 'get out of here'. That was horrible.

The Treasury windows had been smashed and protesters had broken into the Supreme Court building and managed to light a fire inside. Protesters outside bunched around a burning bench to keep warm; the square was blanketed by an ethereal light from a policeman's box recently set alight. Graffiti had been daubed on all available landmarks, including Churchill's statue. *Education for the Masses* one slogan read.

Meanwhile a contingent of protesters had broken out of the kettle and congregated in Trafalgar Square. One had set the square's Christmas tree on fire – granted yearly by the Norwegian city of Oslo to commemorate Britain's role in successfully expelling the German occupation during the Second World War. This warranted another charge by the police to disperse the remaining group. As clocks struck 8 p.m. and fires raged across central London, one kilometre away in

Soho a conflagration soon to make the front covers of many British newspapers was unfolding.

On their way to a Royal Variety Performance at the London Palladium, the car carrying Prince Charles and the Duchess of Cornwall was accosted by protesters on Argyll Street. Paint splattered the car, kicks dented the doors, and the passenger window was cracked.[37] Clarence House said that the passengers were unharmed, if shaken. Students had accosted politicians before, but never the Royal Family. In March 1968 Cambridge students had jumped in front of the car of the then Defence Minister Denis Healey. That protest resulted in five arrests and a discussion in Parliament.[38] Warwick University students egged Margaret Thatcher in 1984 when she came to visit the university. Another protest on campus against Education Secretary Sir Keith Joseph landed the student union with a £30,000 fine.[39] None of these, however, could quite match the affront to British values provided by a placard stick stuck through the heir to the throne's car window. The Queen was 'shocked and disturbed', a high-ranking courtier relayed. 'Her Majesty will not and cannot take sides but she is deeply concerned by the violent scenes … And a divided country is a state of affairs which troubles her heart.'[40] There is no higher point for British protest to reach than the Queen herself. The students had truly shaken the heart of the establishment.

The demonstration ended with a kettle on Westminster Bridge. 'People were panicking around me', James Butler remembers. 'They were really genuinely being crushed. I remember someone saying they were going to fall off the bridge.' After lasting a number of hours cramped against the sides of the bridge in the freezing December cold, the police finally started letting the protesters leave at 11.30 p.m. Craig

Gent describes being 'squashed out of the funnel of coppers with covered faces, saying things like "oh yeah we've won" … and at the bottom there was someone from police intelligence with the camera and a bright light in your face'. 'Anonymous' remembers how the cold on the bridge lasted long after returning home: 'I've been in snowstorms in Northern Scotland, but I've never been that cold … J, my friend, insisted on not paying for the tube, so we got the 341 bus back home. Unfortunately, it didn't come for 30 minutes. I woke up the next day cold right to my core.'

The aftermath of the protest left many seriously shaken. Arianna Tassinari remembers 'quite a lot of us got hurt. One of the SOAS occupiers lost a finger, while others had panic attacks in the kettle on Westminster Bridge. It was pretty intense and quite traumatic.' 'The December 9th demo was the most traumatising experience for my friends', recalled Naiara Bazin. 'One woman was on the floor being kicked by cops, left with bruises on her stomach. Another was left with nightmares about being beaten up by the police – she never got involved again.' Among the Manchester contingent – totalling 450 people brought down in nine coaches – one student had a broken collarbone, another a broken arm and a third a broken ankle. All were caused by police violence. Jamie Woodcock describes how half of the contingent couldn't make the coach back because they had been contained in the kettle. 'We had to find emergency accommodation for 150 students in London', Woodcock recalls. 'We waited for the others in the kettle and then phoned people in the London occupations to put people up. Everyone remembered that when we got back to Manchester. That was the real break with the student union. They said: "if you are in the kettle you are on your own". They left without us.' James Butler suffered a head injury from a police baton:

This cop batons me around the back of the head – I still have a scar to this day. It was only later when I went to take off my hat that I realised it had stuck to my head with blood. Our attempts to get to Parliament didn't work … a friend who works there told me later that 'you could smell the fires inside' … The violence was unbelievable.

MPs couldn't just smell the fires, they could see the clashes from inside the besieged building. Greg Mulholland MP, one of the main figures in the Liberal Democrat rebellion, watched on from his office:

My office is in Portcullis House looking at the Palace of Westminster, so clearly you could see a packed Parliament Square with protesters all below. There was an extraordinary atmosphere. That would have affected everybody and everyone would have been very aware of it all day … I don't think any of us will ever forget them.

Other MPs had a different reaction. Tory MP Christopher Pincher wished to 'commend the actions of the police, which I saw from my office window', against the 'thugs' outside.[41] These words meant little to those students who didn't have lines of armed guards and a pane of glass between them and the police. Rosie Bergonzi, an A-Level student from Brighton, wrote of how her feelings about the police changed after the demonstration:

Right up until that night I had respected the police. I really believed they were there for our protection and that they wanted the good of our citizens. What I witnessed completely destroyed this picture of them. We were treated like cattle, completely stripped of any human decency or rights ... I protested for want of an education, but what I received was a traumatic lesson in police brutality.[42]

Protesters had to wait years for justice. Police Constable Andrew Ott was convicted of knocking out the tooth of William Horner, a student at Royal Holloway, and was sentenced to eight months in prison in May 2015. The evidence showed Ott bragging about assaulting students and goading on his colleagues. Another protester, Alfie Meadows, suffered serious brain injuries after being hit in the head by a police truncheon. He survived only thanks to three twists of fate. With a serious head injury and a developing dizziness, Meadows was reluctantly let out the kettle by the police. Without anyone to accompany him he was forced to wander around Victoria looking for help. As Peter Hallward, a professor at Kingston University recounted:

Alfie's subsequent survival depended on three chance events. If his mother ... hadn't received his phone call and caught up with him soon afterwards, the odds are that he'd have passed out on the street. If they hadn't then stumbled upon an ambulance waiting nearby, his diagnosis could have been fatally delayed. And if the driver of this ambulance hadn't overruled an initial refusal of the A&E department of the Chelsea and Westminster hospital to look at Alfie [because he was a protester], his transfer to the Charing

Cross neurological unit for emergency brain surgery might well have come too late.[43]

The Green Party was one of the only mainstream political parties whose leading members came to the demonstrations and spoke out against the police violence. The Liberal Democrats, usually vocal on questions of civil liberties – notably their opposition to identity cards – were silent on the repression during the protests. Vince Cable claimed that he was largely unaware of the behaviour of the police during the demonstrations: 'We were having to battle this intense wall of hostility around the issue, and to be frank I wasn't actually aware of what was happening on the ground with the policing – I was dealing with the politics of it all in the background.'

In Parliament, Theresa May expressed her 'gratitude to those police officers and commanders who put themselves in harm's way … It was this bravery that enabled this House to engage unhindered in democratic debate.'[44] Newspapers like *The Sun* fed the moral panic: 'We can no longer blame the London riots on a tiny minority. Clearly an organised attempt is under way by anarchists and extremists to undermine our democracy … A national threat demands a national response.'[45] Theresa May did not mention any criticism of police behaviour or acknowledge the numerous injuries and trauma to students:

Some students behaved disgracefully. However, the police assess that the protests were infiltrated by organised groups of hardcore activists and street gangs bent on violence … I want to be absolutely clear that the blame for the violence lies squarely and solely with those who carried it out. The idea advanced by some that police tactics were to blame, when people came armed with sticks, flares, fireworks, stones and snooker balls, is as ridiculous as it is unfair.[46]

Ed Balls, Labour Shadow Home Secretary, continued the attacks: 'All Labour Members also share the Home Secretary's anger and outrage at the way in which last Thursday's legitimate day of action was hijacked by a small but significant minority bent on provocation, violence and criminal damage.' The 'bravery and commitment' of the police officers and their 'professionalism and restraint' were also praised by Balls.[47] Rather than criticise the police for their tactics or the government for their handling of the movement, Balls chose instead to admonish May for the cuts to police numbers. At least one MP pressured May to say at least something about the students: 'is it not sad that the Home Secretary said nothing about them in her statement?' Labour MP Alun Michael asked. The only voice raised to make a direct case for the students was that of the MP for Islington North, Jeremy Corbyn:

> I met a number of students last Thursday evening who were shocked and distressed … Will the Home Secretary have a serious discussion with the Metropolitan Police Commissioner about the use of kettling tactics and corralling people against their will when they wish only to demonstrate peacefully against what they see as – and I agree with them – the monstrous imposition of a fees increase.[48]

Conservative MPs compared the threat posed by the protesters to 'foreign preachers', the troubles in Northern Ireland and the war in Afghanistan. 'My constituents will be incredibly concerned about reports that suggest that some agitators came from overseas countries, such as Latvia and Germany', claimed Robert Halfon, Conservative MP for Harlow.[49] David Cameron said the demonstrators had acted in 'an absolutely feral way'.[50] The Liberal Democrat MP Duncan Hames decried 'malevolent forces' at work.[51] In early January 2011, Scotland Yard's counter-terrorism unit sent an email to all London universities asking that they 'pick up any relevant information that would be helpful to all of us to anticipate possible demonstrations or occupations' and then 'forward it' to them.[52] 'Lecturers are to become informants; their students the enemy within – terrorists', Nina Power wrote.[53] The threat of the 'enemy within' was compared to the enemy without. The threat of the students was seen as comparable to the threat posed by the ongoing 'War on Terror'. The students, unwittingly, had caused not only a headache over tuition fees and education cuts, but had forced a crisis of governance.

Students often felt exasperated by the media portrayal of the protests. Ben Brown, a BBC news anchor, insinuated that Jody McIntyre – a young activist with cerebral palsy, confined to a wheelchair pushed by his brother – was responsible for being twice thrown to the ground by the police and dragged along the floor. Brown, confronting McIntyre on air, suggested that 'wheeling yourself towards the police' could have justified their actions.[54] Figures in the media and in politics lined up to condemn the students and to delegitimise the movement.

The police ramped up their hunt for suspects to prosecute. S.G. remembers his cousins and friends, still at secondary school, were featured on the BBC *Crimewatch* programme. 'Because their faces were on TV, my cousin's school gave him up, whereas the school of my cousin's friend didn't. These were secondary school kids.' A. recalls the post-demonstration analysis at school the next day:

> I remember going to school the next day and having a deep conversation with my history teacher. He said: 'remember this moment here would be remembered throughout time'. We didn't know it at the time, and I just completely disregarded it. But when it came down to it, it was a pretty big moment when it came to the prospects of young people in this country. But having it go against the expectations of the majority of people was a kick in the teeth...

So ended one of the most violent demonstrations in decades, marking the end of the 2010 British student movement.

## The aftermath

The demonstration on December 9th marked a watershed in British politics. Students watched on from the kettle as the vote in Parliament was passed. Only 23 Liberal Democrats rebelled, along with six Conservatives. All 17 Liberal Democrat government ministers voted with the government. All 253 Labour MPs voted against the rise. The government's majority had been reduced from 84 to 21.

Students went into the Christmas holidays without having swung the balance in Parliament. The next student demonstration, on January 29th, was much smaller than in November. Its slogan: 'What Parliament does, the streets can undo.' Split between 'official' and 'unofficial' movements, the demonstration remained fragmented. The movement's energy had been substantially lost in England. It had, however, shaken the government to its core. Students had swept aside their traditional representatives and demanded to be heard directly. Their protests had reached the very heart of the British establishment and forced a debate on the state of the nation. British young people had made a direct and collective intervention into historical events.

# CHAPTER FIVE

# *Occupy, Agitate, Organise*

Attending the SOAS occupation as a journalist for *Newsnight*, Paul Mason was struck by meetings 'conducted in an atmosphere of flat-faced calm'. A prayer area had been set up for Muslim students, while Hardt and Negri's *Multitude*, a Foucault primer and Guy Debord's *Society of the Spectacle* lay on the floor. All indicated an 'obvious but unspoken cultural difference between modern youth movements and those of the past'.[1] The cultural shift was shown in the distaste for 'ideology':

> Anybody who sounds like a career politician, anybody who attempts rhetoric, espouses ideology, or lets their emotions overtake them is greeted with a visceral distaste. There is no ideology driving this movement and no coherent vision of an alternative society ... They realise, in a way previous generations of radicals did not, that emotion-fuelled action, loyalty, mesmeric oratory and hierarchy all come at an overhead cost.[2]

As the voices of participants attest, the reality was both similar and more complex than this description. Underneath the calm exterior, ideological and political divisions formed a hidden subtext. What seemed spontaneous was often meticulously organised. A movement which appeared to be a radical break from the past also felt the weight of past traditions. What at first seemed unprecedented had antecedents in recent memory. The new culture Mason noted was real and tangible, but it wasn't the whole story. This chapter explores the role of organisational and associational cultures in a movement that actively spurned politics with a capital 'P'. To understand the 2010 revolt, understanding how students occupied, agitated and organised is key.

## The occupations

The 24th of November 2010 marked a national day of action by students across the country. Occupiers seized spaces in UCL, Oxford, Cambridge, Royal Holloway College, Plymouth, Warwick, Birmingham, London South Bank, the Slade School of Fine Art, Leeds, Essex, Cardiff, Sheffield, Newcastle, University of the West of England (UWE), Bradford, Bristol and Edinburgh, among others. There were so many occupations that activists found it hard to keep count. Occupations would strike 46 campuses, according to one participant.[3] Occupiers at Newcastle University also turned a 2,000-person demonstration and 'teach-in' by local school, college and university students into a 19-day occupation of the Fine Arts Building.[4] Camden School for Girls in north London organised an overnight occupation. Students made demands on their university managements to speak out against the fee rise and the marketisation of education. From those lasting hours to those lasting months, the occupations were spaces where demonstration stewards were recruited, leaflets were printed, banners were made, flashmobs were organised, and students and staff mobilised.

## Historical precedents

Militants in the late 1960s understood that the appropriation of space was of crucial political importance for student movements.[5] Student activists advocated a theory of 'red bases', where universities could become liberated spaces, outside the values of bourgeois society, from which revolutionary action could be waged. Elements of the 'red base' ethos did re-emerge in some of the occupations and initiatives in the autumn of 2010. Owen Hatherley wrote that 'the certain intensity' of the university occupations lay not in their 'critique of the singularly grotesque millionaires' austerity government, but in their attempt to imagine a new kind of everyday life.'[6] Occupiers in 2010 organised outreach programmes, 'reimagined' education outside 'neoliberal ideology', and liberated space from the strictures of the market. Initiatives in 2010 and its aftermath included the Reimagine the University organized by the 'Really Open University', the Camp for Education at the University of West England (UWE), the University of Utopia in Lincoln, the Free School at LSE, the University for Strategic Optimism at Goldsmiths, the Bloomsbury Fightback project, the Really Free School occupation, the Teach-Out and Teach-Ins at Oxford, SOAS and UCL, and the Arts Against the Cuts in Tate Britain (which delayed the Turner Prize). Like in the late 1960s, students were using space to reimagine life outside of the market.

The occupations' prefigurative political feeling reflected, in language and action, student movements of the past. In

2010, however, students lacked the confident expectation of an imminent revolutionary rupture. Closer to home, the experiments of the 'free university' and 'teach-in' had parallels with both the occupations of Hornsey and Hull in 1968 and the July 1967 Dialectics of Liberation conference at London's Roundhouse. Situationism – a transnational artistic, political and intellectual movement from the late 1950s to the early 1970s which developed a critique of capitalism based on a mixture of Marxism and surrealism – became an ideological accessory for a certain (small but vocal) section of the protestors.[7] Consciously or unconsciously, students in 2010 followed in longer historical traditions.

## Gaza occupations 2009

Yet the 2010 occupations did not have to look only to the 1960s for antecedents. In early 2009, thousands of students had occupied lecture theatres and administration buildings at over 20 UK campuses in opposition to the Israeli invasion of Gaza in 'Operation Cast Lead'. The universities occupied included LSE, Essex, King's College London, Birmingham, Sussex, Warwick, Manchester Metropolitan, Manchester, Oxford, Leeds, Cambridge, Sheffield Hallam, Bradford, Nottingham, Queen Mary, Strathclyde, Newcastle, Kingston, Goldsmiths and Glasgow.[8] Students demanded the disinvestment of their universities from the arms trade; a promise to provide scholarships for Palestinian students; a pledge to send books and unused computers to Palestine; and a condemnation by their universities of the Israeli attacks.[9] Caught unawares, university authorities in most of the affected universities accepted at least one of the students' demands.

'For decades, student activism has been in the doldrums in this country ... But that may be about to change', a journalist from *The Times* wrote of the movement.[10] Nina Power agreed on the link between 2009 and 2010. 'After the numerous university occupations in solidarity with the Palestinians over Operation Cast Lead in 2009', she said, 'there was a willingness to occupy in 2010.' There were precedents not simply in what 'students were doing' but also in the reaction of the state, which 'had used charges of Violent Disorder against the Palestine solidarity protesters'. As Sai Englert remembered, Sussex University went into occupation a week before the first national demo on November 10, 'fairly self-consciously influenced by the Gaza occupations of 2009 ... with an eye on the French model [of shutting down the university system]'. Jamie Woodcock, an undergraduate student in Manchester in 2009, participated in a 31-day occupation in solidarity with those in Gaza:

Occupations became a thing that you didn't just read about in books of the 1960s, but tactics you tried and won with. You figured out which rooms were worth taking, how to take them, how to get people involved ... A lot of the skills and techniques [for 2010] were learnt during that occupation. We had to negotiate with the university management, as well as learn how to escalate things, make demands, and how to hold national demos on our campus ... We found the places that if you occupied the management didn't care, as you weren't disrupting anything. Because we had tried it in practice before, when it came to 2010 it was much easier to make an argument for them. It was a training ground, essentially.

I think it is really important not to forget the effect that having victories has on peoples' confidence. Ultimately, we won all our demands apart from one ... There was a feeling that you could have power over an institution like Manchester that has 50,000 students and staff. That was incredibly important – an important learning process of struggle, even though they were over quite different issues and not everyone transferred between the two ... Starting the story in 2010 does a big disservice to the victories and experience of the movement before that.

No movement emerges from nothing. Experiences and skills learnt in previous times re-emerge in new contexts. The 2010 movement against tuition fees, organised around a purely 'national issue', was deeply influenced by past movements of international solidarity.

*Starting the occupations*

Each occupation started when like-minded students came together in action. The UCL occupation emerged from a meeting where the tensions between the spirit and practices of old and new left were at their most acute. The Education Activist Network (EAN) – a student and lecturer anti-cuts organisation with deep connections to the Socialist Workers Party (SWP) – held a meeting in King's College London on November 15th to discuss where the movement would go after Millbank. Mark Bergfeld, a leading activist in EAN, describes the meeting:

A few days after the student demonstration on November 10th we had a big hall booked in King's College London, in a classic top-down socialist meeting. I had never seen such a packed meeting ... You had people sitting in the balconies, you had people in the galleries. People were sitting all over the floor and the stage ... The spirit was really crazy. But we absolutely messed it up. The SWP cadres, EAN people, everyone messed it up. We didn't understand – we effectively couldn't articulate what had just happened. Millbank took us by surprise. We had a line of speakers set-up for that meeting prior to the demonstration, and we just continued with business as usual. We didn't understand that people were coming here to organise and discuss collectively. They didn't want to be lectured to by anyone – especially not lecturers from the UCU! We didn't capture the anti-authoritarian mood that came out of the Millbank protests ... We saw it in front of us, but with every minute that the meeting passed it just slipped away.

The meeting provided the spur to create the UCL occupation. As Ben Beach explains:

EAN had only booked the room for two hours. About four [speakers] stood up and said the same tropes, and wouldn't shut up with these banal speeches. So we had half an hour of floor-time to actually discuss 'what next'. And the SWP chair was just picking fellow SWP people to speak ... It was so frustrating. I was on the verge of tears. And they began to say: 'well the meeting is drawing to a close' and everyone started to get angry. But they finished the meeting up. And everyone was supposed to leave at this point – about 150 to 200 people. I was livid. So I stood on a chair and said 'the most important thing we can get from this meeting is to find each other, I'm from UCL, where are you from?'

And then people were responding 'I'm from Queen Mary', 'I'm from LSE', and so on. I found a group of about eight people. We arranged to have a plotting meeting in the UCL basement, and had decided there and then that we were going to occupy the university ... It became quite obvious to us that there needed to be a new way of doing things, and that nobody was really offering that to us.

Not every university occupation started like the one in UCL. SOAS, one of the more traditionally radical universities, was one of the first to be occupied following Millbank. Arianna Tassinari describes how, following a more traditional model, SOAS students wanted to have official backing from the student union for their action, both to raise awareness of the movement and to gain democratic legitimacy for their action. No such meeting was held at Oxford. Students there had trouble deciding on a place to occupy. In Oxford, a demonstration circled around Radcliffe Square before entering the Bodleian Library's Radcliffe Camera. The occupation of the most iconic library in the university – during exam time – still makes participant James Butler 'swing back and forth between if it was the right thing to do'. The decision on where to occupy 'was difficult', Nick Evans remembers. 'Some thought it was important in symbolic terms – in terms of pressure on authorities – others for opening up knowledge to different people'.

At other universities protestors flinched at occupying student spaces, instead choosing buildings that would exert the maximum pressure on university managements. At 7 a.m. on November 26th in Cambridge, 50 students assembled in a room at a local student-run café with bike locks and sleeping bags. All were prepared to occupy the Old Schools, which housed the offices of the university Vice Chancellor and other senior officials. 'Four groups of three went ahead with locks in their hands and took the building, locking open the gates; 40 people with sleeping bags ran through', remembered Naiara Bazin.

Craig Gent recounts the experiences at Royal Holloway, where students occupied 'the most opulent corridor in the Founder's Building', where guests are taken to be impressed. 'On the first night we had about 100 people there, and on the second night we called a party ... it was only supposed to last 24 hours. Royal Holloway had never had an occupation before, only a couple of people had been at the LSE occupation around Gaza in 2009 ... People didn't know how to react to it.' There were three separate occupations at Royal Holloway, including at the university building in Bloomsbury's Bedford Square.

Not every occupation started as well. Many didn't go exactly to plan. On the University of Birmingham campus it was 'difficult-slash-impossible to get much going for very long', remembered Malia Bouattia. At Warwick University on November 24th, a march of over 200 stormed the Arts Theatre and started an occupation. Ruth recalls 'it was all a bit of a disaster':

> The lecture theatre didn't have toilets or food. There were lots of people, but many hadn't planned to stay. Only about 30 did. We didn't know that the air conditioning would come on during the night, and it was absolutely freezing. The university didn't let people in, but let them out. If you needed to go to the toilet you had to go out, so some people urinated in a bucket. Eventually there were only a handful

of us left there in the morning. Some food had arrived, from the Warwick Business School – from the industrial relations unit, from Marxists who study labour relations! We didn't have the numbers so we marched out and declared a victory, and started planning for future events.

Some occupations were evicted fairly swiftly. At the Bodleian Library occupation in Oxford, late-night discussions with librarians who had stayed overnight to guard the books were interrupted the next morning by the violent entry of the police. James Butler remembers officers 'kicked down the partition wall under the library' to evict the students. Only a couple of students were called to interview with senior university staff, but 'fortunately', this being Oxford, 'one of those people said that if they were to resort to disciplinary action then they would go to so and so at *The Guardian* … and so they backed off'. The movement in Warwick and Oxford didn't end there, however.

In the weeks after Millbank, university managements across the country had to face up to a new reality. Student occupations were back.

*Finding a structure*

Each occupation had to decide on how to organise their newly liberated space. All around the country the first 'general meeting' of the occupation played host to fierce debates on how to structure its democratic procedures. Much like the Occupy movement – which was to steal the headlines in 2011 after the occupation of Zuccotti Park outside the New York Stock Exchange – students in Britain were concerned that the democracy inside their movement did not reflect that of the wider political system. To root democracy at the level of everyday experience, occupations were structured around direct and open participation. They were imprinted with the same ethos as other movements across the world. Dario Azzellini and Maria Sitrin show how the movements of the squares and experiments in popular democracy since 2008 have been marked, like those in 2010, with this partic-ipatory spirit.[11] Movements in Spain, Argentina, Greece and Venezuela used similar open assemblies based on horizontal-ism and the principle of self-organisation. The representative failure of Britain's major political parties spurred students on to create their own alternative polity on their campuses.

Yet as soon as they entered the occupied spaces tensions between different political traditions inside the student body became apparent. The debate often polarised between those advocating non-hierarchical 'consensus' decision-making, open 'general meetings' and self-organised 'working groups' which anyone could join, and those who advocated a more structured approach in which voting replaced consensus-building for resolving intractable disputes. The occupation at UCL exhibited many of these tensions. Close to Parliament and the BBC's headquarters, and with a brilliantly organised media strategy and a consensus decision-making structure, the occupation would become a paradigm for the British student occupations. Aaron Bastani describes the process through which the democratic structure was created:

I'd say 60 per cent of the people involved had no activist experience or inheritance, although the organisers who made the call for the occupation did have activist experience

... The prevalence of consensus is purely because of the vanguardism of two climate activists who took control of the meeting early on and suggested the model.

The same process occurred in Cambridge where a minority of ex-Climate Camp activists played formative roles. The Camp for Climate Action, or Climate Camp as it is popularly known, was started in 2006 to protest inaction on climate change. After occupations at Drax Power Station and Heathrow, the camp was disbanded in 2011 as its participants moved into other campaigns. Many activists trained in the movement were involved in the 2010 occupations, bringing with them their skills and experience in organising spaces of non-violent direct action. As Naiara Bazin explains, 'those [involved] in Climate Camp, and ... the people [who] had gone into occupation over the massacre in Gaza' brought their experiences into the occupation. 'There was a massive division between the anarcho-types and Climate Camp people and the SWP', Bazin recalled. 'There was a lot of tension, but in the end we won [an occupation run on consensus decision-making]'. Not all the students accepted the structure, which included 'twinkling' both hands in the air if you agreed with a point (rather than the traditional clapping), and crossing both arms if you wished to block a motion. There were some students who refused to abide by the rules, Bazin remembered. 'It was quite funny really.'

For UCL student Ben Beach, the intricate processes of consensus-building posed problems: 'It became apparent that there was no unifying ideology in the room; which was a problem as new democratic forms, not previously present on campus, meant four hour meetings.' UCL occupier Alessandro

Furlotti admitted to being a member of the Conservative Party. 'I'm not left-wing but I firmly believe these cuts on education are unjust', he said.[12] Maintaining an occupation based on consensus decision-making with political allegiances spanning from the Tories to revolutionary communists was a difficult task. For first-year undergraduate Hannah Sketchley, many of the debates in the UCL occupation – 'between more anti-structuralist, anarchically minded people and more Trotskyist-influenced people' – passed her by. 'If I was more factionally savvy at the time I would have had more of an idea of what was going on but at the time it felt that there was just a lot of very strange arguments that I only half followed', Sketchley remembered. Ben Beach admits that 'there were barriers to participation': the 'reputation of UCL being that you sort of had to be a militant communist to be involved … people had this perception that they couldn't get involved'. The problems of the organisational model chosen became apparent early on, argues Sketchley:

> The occupation fell into the trap that your prominence in the occupation came down to stamina more than ideas. And there were several loud noticeable voices – those who were there all the time; because of that people listened to them … Working groups were largely autonomous which meant that there was less recall process, meaning the occupation was quite atomised.

Unlike in student movements of the past, the demands of the occupations were not the key mobilising factor for participants. Most occupations failed to win their demands – the reversal of planned cuts, fee increases, and statements by university managements to condemn the changes. Clearly, however, certain occupations did gain local victories. As activist Jo Casserly noted, 'some universities – such as [London] South Bank, won a number of their demands'.[13] The focus and tone of the demands were influenced by the fact that students saw university management as directly complicit in the policies advocated by the Browne Review. 'There was a sense at the time of an apocalyptic mood. Public education was going down the drain and the university would watch it happen', Nick Evans recalls. Few interviewees mentioned the demands of the occupations on university management. Naiara Bazin couldn't remember what the occupation's demands were – 'I don't know if we ever met with university management, but I may not have been aware of it.' Ariana Tassinari described the negotiations with SOAS management as 'semi-farcical'. SOAS occupiers, like many students in 2010, had an aversion to negotiations and demands, which would only legitimise powerholders and precious waste time. They did not go as far as some Cambridge anarchists had in 1968 when they 'proposed a blank piece of paper as a manifesto for the Revolutionary Socialist Student Federation in opposition to what they called a trivial set of slogans'.[14] The political goal of the occupiers was to pressurise the university as a shortcut to pressurising the state.

## The left

The impact of far-left groups on the organisation and internal culture of the occupations was not uniform. Much depended on the size of the groups on campus, the personalities involved, and their previous organising record. Some of the tensions between left organisations and many non-aligned, new or anarchist-influenced students revolved around traditions and styles of organising. The student revolt's spirit sat uneasily with organised politics. Arianna Tassinari noted that 'at SOAS there was a tendency against too much organisation; this spontaneous attitude that made things a mess much of the time'. Yet this didn't mean that there was a total antipathy to 'emotion-fuelled action, loyalty or hierarchy'. Many of the occupation's leading figures were members of disciplined far-left groups. As Tassinari explains:

> Only one group organised inside the occupation, Counterfire. Acting as an organised bloc ... they could intervene in a political situation that we, as a heterogeneous mass, coming from different places, with undefined anarcho-tendencies, couldn't do. We didn't like the idea of an 'intervention' in a meeting to get it to go their way, yet the rest of us didn't have the organisation to counter it ... We were all new to politics, trying to make it work.

The occupation at Leeds saw some of the most serious disputes. One journalist witnessed scenes far removed from the 'calm' SOAS occupation observed by Paul Mason:

> Longhaired and big-booted, revolutionary socialist Luke stands up in front of a meeting at the Leeds university occupation, and prepares to speak. 'Comrades...', Luke begins – and, from the back of this lecture theatre filled with 200 undergraduates, school students, trade unionists and parents, comes an instant, shouted response. 'DON'T CALL ME COMRADE.' 'We can't afford to alienate people

with different theoretical backgrounds', says one speaker.
'We can run this country by ourselves – we don't need
capitalism to do it for us', says the next. 'Hello everybody,
I'm from Greece' gets a cheer from a doctrinaire section
of the crowd, the postgraduate who responds with 'I don't
have a political allegiance' wins applause from another.[15]

Although activists from left-wing groups played leading roles
in the movement, the 2010 revolt could be corralled by no
organisation. It set its own agenda.

*Occupational cultures*

Among the most abiding memories for participants was the
vibrant cultural and associational life of the occupations. They
were more than instruments of leverage against university
managements; they were also experiments in different ways
of living and social interaction. The occupation at Cambridge
University exemplified the fledgling occupational cultures
spreading over British campuses. The ten-day occupation was
one of the largest and most vibrant in the country, with over
200 students regularly meeting in the occupied Old Schools
site for meetings and events. Naiara Bazin remembers the
internal life of the occupation:

There were media skills shares, direct action training –
Climate Camp people were building the capacitates of
people like me who didn't have much experience beforehand
… I think still to this date that everyone I know would say
that it was the most incredible, magical, inspiring political
experience of their lives.

Not only universities were occupied. Many in the 2010 student generation participated in the roaming occupation called the 'Really Free School', which began in January 2011. The collective was named after Coalition Education Secretary Michael Gove's plans for 'Free Schools' to be set up and run by parents autonomous of the state system. After occupying film director Guy Ritchie's multimillion-pound unoccupied property in Fitzrovia, the Really Free School organised a daily schedule of events open to the public – including films, workshops, discussions, poetry nights, workshops (on 'building barricades' and 'agitprop'), and even an 'erotic rope-tying skill share', Aadam Muuse remembered. The Really Free School was a formative experience for college student Muuse. Eventually evicted in February, the occupiers attended their court hearing wearing masks bearing the face of Vinnie Jones, the ex-footballer turned actor who had appeared in Guy Ritchie's film *Lock, Stock and Two Smoking Barrels*. Before the Coalition government changed the squatting laws in 2012 to make these experiments harder, many squatted spaces and social centres provided a 'hub to organise, rest, build community', and facilitate political education. For Ben Beach one of the most important outcomes of the occupations was a culture of radical friendship:

It was an incredibly special time. The place was absolutely humming with raw energy. Collisions of bodies and organisations *felt* new … It was all done through consent, and things were done on the basis of being friends: a radical friendship.

The occupations offered liminal spaces where students could develop new ways of organising social interaction outside the logic of marketised education. Government and university intransigence cut these experiments short.

## Intellectuals and the occupations

Given the preponderance of university students in the revolt, it is no surprise that students and academics framed the experiences of the occupations through theory. Danny Hayward noted that Edinburgh University's ('Deleuzian') occupation was 'the most energetic in disseminating propaganda about the "swarm" quality of the student movement'.[16] Jacob Bard-Rosenberg described some of the theoretical influences of the 'Bloomsbury Fightback' collective, which arose out of an occupation in Bedford Square: 'Many shared theoretical interests like Marx, Italian 1970s Marxists, *Operaismo*, Pannekoek; a shared feminist critique of Leninist parties and an appreciation for poetic modernism ... It was an attempt to create a politics that broke from politics.' James Butler also remembers

reading a lot of Italian stuff, on their late 1960s and 1970s student movement, at the time. We were running a *Capital* Reading Group, reading some early Antoni Negri – the *Books for Burning* stuff[17] ... *The Unseen*,[18] which was passed around a lot of squats at the time like the Really Free School. I think that book informed some of the political culture at the time. There was a millenarian aspect to it all.

The Goldsmiths occupation offered one of the clearest examples of the interplay between theory and activity in the student protests. One Goldsmiths occupier, who wished to remain anonymous, saw the problems posed by elements of the 'academic left' who aimed at determining the occupation's strategy:

There was an academic left – a well read, moustache-twisting group – which wanted to apply these very abstract concepts onto a group of people who were just starting to think. It got shut down by a couple of loudmouth academics who insisted that the library was a 'social factory' [which needed to be completely shut off to students]. If you do believe that the university is a social factory, the best way to argue for that is not to quote a French academic and then shout at people for being scabs when they don't believe you. Everyone else was like: 'let's occupy the library as it's a useful place to organise, but let's allow people in to use the books, and invite school students in 24 hours a day'. The first meeting had around 500 people, but within three or four days it was down to 70 to 80 people.

The different intellectual strands present in the occupations depended on the political composition of the occupiers. What is clear is that there was a noted prevalence of anarchist, 'autonomist' and Situationist literature, as well as the more traditional literature of the Marxist classics and poststructuralism disseminated by the different left groups and university courses. Although on a smaller scale, British students followed the example of those in 1968 who read and appropriated theory produced outside Britain (especially from continental Europe) for domestic political ends.

*Outreach*

The occupations were not spaces solely for university students, but became hubs of community organising that bridged the gap between school and university. The links between them were not without their problems. North London college student Kieran Sutton was conscious of the age gap: 'university students at the time seem to me like adults – big adults. That was part of the problem at the time.' Joana Ramiro remembers how 'people were a bit dismissive about how school students would form their own opinions, about how we had to speak to them not with them'. Huw Lemmey recalled how 'six anarchists' volunteered for the outreach working group of the Goldsmiths occupation, while the Twitter working group had eighteen. The former was still able to organise hundreds of school students from Lewisham College to attend the demonstrations with the university occupiers. Aadam Muuse, at St John Cass Sixth Form College in east London, also noted the constructive relationship between Queen Mary University students and college students. Helping to leaflet on the days of the demonstrations, and walking with students to Mile End tube to go to central London, 'they didn't try to impose anything on us or tell us what to do. They provided bodies and reassurance.' There was also support between different colleges, with Muuse going 'out to leaflet Tower Hamlets College'. In Newcastle, university students chaired meetings with pupils from nine local schools. 'It was the young people who decided what action to take', 16-year-old school student occupier Saskia Neivig told a *Guardian* journalist. She continued: 'The students said: "The second day of action is for young people to decide what to do. We'll help you out in whatever way, but the schoolchildren –

it's their generation that'll be affected."[19] Kieran Sutton saw the role of 'organised lefties' as important, but not critical, in encouraging school students to walk out:

People were angry and started to go on protests and walkouts, but also there were organised lefties going to the colleges and asking: 'why aren't you coming out?' ... People were going to walk out anyway – but it was a confidence boost: a shot in the arm, a guide ... There was an osmosis or bleeding into each other. All four of my friends [who participated in the protests] slept at each of the occupations in Bloomsbury. There was a hubbub of young people around that area.

Ben Beach was less convinced that the links with further education colleges were successful: 'there was relatively no meaningful relationship ... I mean we couldn't even work out how to organise higher education students let alone further education students'. The problem in relating to school and college students was a question not just of age but of class and ethnicity. School students certainly wouldn't find any Grime raves – a main staple of the demonstrations – at UCL. According to Michael Chessum, 'the UCL occupation, being populated by posh white people, would go back and listen to loud classical music ... drinking port and red wine ... Not everyone was a working-class, black, further education student from North London.'

For Mark Bergfeld, the grievances of the school students were completely underestimated by all sections of the movement. University students and school and college students approached the movement from very different starting points. Student organisations focused solely on education issues couldn't tap into the spontaneous anger produced by more general grievances. As Bergfeld recalled:

> There was a clear cleavage in the agendas and between the languages that the different protestors spoke. The organisations which had been founded prior to Millbank were concentrating on education issues and university issues which didn't totally interest these people ... They weren't represented by the student unions, they weren't represented by the political organisations and parties ... they weren't being represented by anyone. They were representing no one but themselves. It developed this emancipatory character of 'we don't have a political voice, so we're going to smash shit up [to make ourselves heard]'.

This speaks to the experiences of Shereen Prasad's school friends from Hackney, many of whom didn't attend the protests. She thought that the movement 'wasn't inclusive enough of school students' who had come to the demonstrations in their uniforms. For many of her friends, education had never been viewed 'as a big deal'. There were deeper grievances at play. 'Yes, they hated David Cameron, but they hated him not because he trebled fees, but for so many more reasons':

> Most of the kids I went to school with weren't even going to go to college, let alone university. They either went into apprenticeships that led to nothing, some have kids and work in retail, some are dead, some are in university, some went to college then didn't go to university. It was never about education, as the education system just never worked

for them … It was just another part of life off limit to us …
It wasn't the first time they had been attacked.

The biggest sentiment in deprived neighbourhoods with
lots of gang violence is 'fuck the system' and 'fuck the police'.
They knew that the system didn't work for them. When the
government turned around and said 'we are going to raise
fees to discourage you from going to university', my friends
turned around and said 'we always knew that it was shit
anyway, there's no point fighting it'. The main battle for
them – for us – was to exist. Not just against the police, but
against each other, against poverty. For them it was either
'fuck the system' or you become a part of it – you are either a
millionaire CEO or nothing. There was no middle way.

They hated the police, not because they were beating
up protesters, but because they had beaten up their friends
and treated them like animals. For them it was like: 'let's go
and get one up on these people. This is our time to do it.' It
was never about 'we need to do this to fight for education'.
It was 'let's do it now as we can probably get away with it
now as there are so many people they couldn't catch us'.
It is hard to argue with that. You can't make them care. I
couldn't convince them as the education system was built
to fail them.

Outreach also meant leaving the occupations to carry out
'direct action' to raise the profile of the movement and
highlight the problem of tax avoidance. Occupiers from the
London occupations joined up with UK Uncut to protest Sir
Philip Green's tax avoidance and support for austerity at the
flagship Topshop store on Oxford Street. A 'teach-out' was
held at Euston train station on the morning of December 9th.

For Ruth, it was an 'incredibly powerful teach-out', disrupting the everyday working of the city with a large discussion about free education. The occupations in 2010 were developing into spaces that transcended the tuition fees issue, turning into more general assaults on austerity politics.

In many cases students were also able to construct meaningful relationships with workers on and off campus, as had those in the last great student rebellions. Some occupations were precipitated by student-worker solidarity. The occupation at UWE from November 22nd was spurred on by the tuition fee increase and the 'university management's decision to effectively demote up to 80 principal lecturers, readers and professors as part of an ongoing program of cuts at the University'.[20] Both students and academics were targets of a similar government strategy to overhaul education. Solidarity didn't just mean bridging the gap to academics, but also making connections outside the university. Kieran Sutton and a couple of school friends made the journey to Euston Fire Station to 'ask for a brazier for one of our pickets outside of college':

They [the fire fighters] were fully on it, but we hadn't given them enough time. They were good about it. 'You are the spark' – 'we are trying to save our jobs ... You are a kid – if you can do it, so can we', they said. I remember talking to this big dude and being like 'rah, am I an inspiration to you? Are you serious? You're a big man.'

A nascent movement was emerging that had the potential not only to mobilise hundreds of thousands of students in defence of their education, but also to show that the struggle over fees was starting to overflow the education system.

## Social media

What made 2010 distinct from previous student movements was its use of social media. Demonstrations around the country could be built in a matter of seconds using a Facebook event. Tweets could report on police violence or issue calls for solidarity in real time. Online blogs offered spaces for analysis outside the mainstream media. British students adopted these new media of communication for their own ends. The movements that were to blossom from 2011, including the Egyptian revolution, the 15-M movement in Spain, Occupy Wall Street and Iceland's Kitchenware Revolution, all used internet-based social networks to facilitate their growth and consolidation. Formed outside traditional party structures and suspicious of mainstream media, these movements were networked, organic, 'leaderless' and dependent on an interplay between internet communications as well as physical mass meetings facilitated by the seizure of physical space.

For Huw Lemmey, social media was more than just an organising tool for the movement, but fed a feeling 'that there were loads of voices that were equal'. Opened up through online platforms, space had been created to organise outside of the traditional 'old left' practices based on campaigns (or 'fronts'), public meetings, conferences and weekly newspapers. As Lemmey notes:

Social media was really important for being able to organise without those big monolithic organisations. Rather than loads of people turning up to the same demonstration under the same banner, there were so many different messages. That made it much more exciting compared to what was happening beforehand.

Aadam Muuse and his friends could 'mobilise through conversations, Blackberry Messenger, Facebook messages' to build a walkout at their school in east London. Participants interviewed after the UWE occupation recounted that 'different things work differently – Facebook within the UWE, encrypted email lists within the core occupation, Twitter between occupations, YouTube for wider society'.[21] Although started in the digital sphere through mass demonstrations publicised online, the move to occupying culturally or politically important urban spaces in the 2010 protests presaged the new social movements of 2011. The student revolt prefigured many of the new tactics of the later movements.

The UCL occupation was the most fitting harbinger of a new 'mass self-communication'. The quality of the digital media strategy in the UCL occupation was noted by students, journalists and politicians. 'UCL had a much slicker media presence than us at SOAS' noted Arianna Tassinari. UCL's Twitter account attracted more than three times as many followers (3908), as second-place Edinburgh (1119).[22] Manchester, SOAS, Newcastle and Cambridge together had more than 750, while Royal Holloway, South Bank and Warwick universities had small followings of around 70. UCL's Twitter followers numbered more than 60 per cent of all the other occupations combined, as well as producing almost 30 per cent of the tweets created. The top three accounts (UCL, Edinburgh and SOAS) 'produced almost as many tweets

(7036) as the rest of the occupation network combined'.[23] Ben Beach recounts John McDonnell MP telling the occupation they 'had a better digital media campaign than all the major political parties'. The UCL occupation seemed to encapsulate the 'networked space between the digital space and the urban space'.[24]

The confluence of the mass movement and new technologies is best encapsulated in the example of Sukey – a computer program to prevent 'kettling' on demonstrations. Taking its name from a nursery rhyme, 'Polly put the kettle on, Sukey take it off again', the program was the invention of recently politicised computer programmers. Through information gathered from individual protesters – like tweets and texts – a GPS live-map of the London protests was created, accessible for anyone with a smartphone. Tweets reporting kettle and protester locations were aggregated back at Sukey HQ. This new technology could become a 'double-edged sword', according to Nina Power. 'Sitting through the trials' of protesters after the movement, Power saw how 'the police were also mining the same information' used by platforms like Sukey. 'If you're not careful they will use the same material against you, without hesitation. There's a warning there.' New technology could be appropriated by both police and protesters.

Reviewing the literature on May 1968, Kristin Ross has challenged the 'geographical reduction of the sphere of activity to Paris, more specifically to the Latin Quarter' – which undervalues the diversity of experiences.[25] The UCL occupation, and the area around Bloomsbury more generally, was the space most resembling the Latin Quarter in 2010. Whereas those at the SOAS occupation compromised 'mainly SOAS people, you had lots of others come to UCL from the outside. It became a focal point', noted Arianna Tassinari. Mark Bergfeld sounded a note of caution: 'The UCL occupation was the most impressive because they had the media links which all the other occupations didn't have.' The portrayal of UCL as 'epitomising the new politics' underemphasised the fact that 'the old left and the new left, through different organisations and different structures, existed side by side and were in contention with each other'.

The 2010 student movement would have existed without the internet. Mass movements of British students have successfully organised mass campaigns with popular participation without online platforms. In 1971, the NUS claimed to have mobilised 450,000 of the 500,000 students in Britain, in a university boycott against the then Education Secretary Margaret Thatcher's attack on student union autonomy.[26] The numbers involved in 2010, on the other hand, were much smaller. Hundreds (if not thousands) of UCL students attended the occupation, but nowhere near a majority directly participated online or offline. In the early 1970s, students won without the internet, while in 2010 they lost. Although use of social media sustained the movement and allowed its rapid expansion, it was neither the cause of the movement nor guaranteed it success.

*Mainstream media*

The importance of social media in the student revolt did not make mainstream media irrelevant. Students and politicians sought to use traditional media channels to promote their views, while editors and producers looked to cover the protests. Perceptions of the protests for the wider public were mediated through newspapers and television as much as social media. Debates in the House of Commons days after the December 9th protest were infused with references to sensational newspaper stories. From newspapers to television and radio, students were constantly in the news – even if this focused heavily on violent scenes during the protests. 'You sent a letter into a newspaper and they ran it, you pitched an article and they would take it', remembered Michael Chessum. The debate between Clare Solomon, Aaron Porter and Jeremy Paxman on *Newsnight* on November 10th exemplified the divisions that would be present during subsequent protests, and the role of traditional media in shaping perceptions. Just as students found it hard to keep the mainstream debate focused on tuition fees and education cuts rather than 'public order', so too ministers in the Coalition found it hard to shift the focus from the Liberal Democrats. David Willetts felt he couldn't actually explain the policy of tuition fees in television interviews because of the media narrative about the Liberal Democrat's broken promise:

> The media was around the poor Liberal Democrats, so when you did media interviews they weren't saying: 'why should students pay £9,000?' They would say: 'Mr Willetts, the Liberal Democrats have lied to them [the students], what would you say to them?' So trying to get 30 seconds at the end to explain how the system worked was a bonus.

The ability to organise and propagate through social media did not mean the end of traditional media's relevance. Participants on both sides still understood the importance of utilising both.

## Conclusion

The Christmas break presented the final coup de grâce for the university occupations, breaking the spine of the movement. The occupations were organising hubs from which to conduct outreach to workers and school students; fast-track finishing schools for activists; cauldrons of competing ideas, organisations and traditions; points of pressure and leverage against university managements; centres of cultural and intellectual exchange; liberated spaces in which students wished to prefigure a new kind of society. All the contradictions and tensions of the movement at large could be found crystallised in the occupations.

The organisational practices and cultures of the 2010 student revolt presaged many future social movements across the world. From theory to aesthetics to organisational strategies, older traditions were appropriated for twenty-first-century revolt. Radical experiments with new technologies and aesthetics did not mean that past traditions had no place in the movement. Its spontaneity did not mean organisation and leadership were no longer central concerns. What seemed to emerge from nothing had been prefigured by past struggles. The movement refuses easy generalisation. Janus-faced, the 2010 student revolt looked to both the past and the future.

# CHAPTER SIX

# Why Did the Students Lose?

Just as student movements can explode seemingly out of nowhere, they can decline as quickly as they emerged. Student movements go up like a rocket and down like a stick, as the saying goes. The movement of 2010 was no different. Coming almost exactly a month after the Millbank demonstration, the vote in Parliament on December 9th dealt a critical blow. Without romanticising the movement or straying into nostalgia, accounting for its outcome is necessary. The movement's split into official and unofficial sections, the unprecedented levels of police repression, the lack of political champions in Parliament, paper solidarity from academics and trade unionists, deep-rooted demobilisation amongst the student body, and failures in strategy – all contributed to the movement's defeat. The intransigence of the Coalition government, however, offers the most compelling reason for why the students lost. To paraphrase Margaret Thatcher, there was no alternative to austerity. Austerity realism trumped all.

## The Coalition is not for turning

Why the government refused to change course, even under sustained pressure, is best explained through the voices of those making the decisions. In retrospect, Vince Cable saw the economic crisis and the spending commitments of the previous Labour government as making a serious reform to higher education 'inevitable'. David Willetts argued that 'there was pressure to bring down public spending, and I wanted to do that without reducing the unit of resource for students on their education'. The logic of austerity and a transformation of the higher education system were inextricably linked. 'What were they [the student protesters] going to convince us of?', Cable asked. 'You know we had a real world problem of financial crisis and spending priorities – it wasn't clear to me what we were to do about it.' He continued:

> The reason why it was inevitable was that we were faced with a Spending Review in the autumn. I had inherited from Peter Mandelson a commitment to cut the department by 25 per cent. We knew if Labour had come back they would have done that. The view in the civil service was that we should take the money out of further education ... I was determined not to go down that road ... I don't think there was any risk of the government losing the vote ... You can't be in government and pretend you aren't in it when something unpopular has to happen ... If the vote was lost then the policy would have been reworked.

Students on the ground quickly understood the kind of power they were confronting. Kieran Sutton learned, through struggling in his college, that 'politics was not about the power of the argument but the argument of power'. For Nina Power, there was little else the movement could have done differently in the face of such a determined government: 'I think the political will of the Tories to pursue their austerity programme meant that they needed to get this victory ... I don't think the movement failed because of a lack of will by students or future students ... I don't think it failed as much as it was deliberately crushed.'

The balance of forces between the different parties allowed few openings. One of the most serious headaches for the Conservatives came from the party's right-wing backbenchers. On the evening before the vote on December 9th, David Cameron and George Osborne met with 'up to ten' potential Tory rebels, mainly on the party's right-wing, in an attempt to win their loyalty for the next day.[1] Peter Bone, Conservative MP for Wellingborough and member of the executive of the 1922 Committee of Tory backbenchers, threatened to rebel over the Coalition settlement: 'This isn't about tuition fees. I am a Conservative, I am not a coalitionist.'[2]

The focus of the NUS's lobbying was still the Liberal Democrats. For Aaron Porter, the 'parliamentary map was such that if enough Liberal Democrats backed the changes, then it would pass. I can't think of any other actions or campaign tasks that could have defeated the policy.' Once leading figures in the party began to side with the government – breaking the pledge they had not supported from the start – the issue was all but settled. Porter continued:

As soon as Vince Cable, the Secretary of State, was willing to endorse £9,000 fees I struggle to see how we could have beaten it ... The preference of the Liberal Democrats for staying in government rather than stopping the motion was what undid us. Everything else – the tactics of lobbying against the tactic of protests... – was inconsequential after the Liberal Democrats had made up their minds.

The reason why the government stubbornly persevered with its policy lies less with parliamentary intrigue and short-term feuds than with 'austerity realism'. The public debt incurred through the bail-out of the private banking system in 2008 needed to be paid off, even if this was by future generations of students with no culpability for the crisis. What made the 2010 student revolt so dangerous for the government was that a policy that was framed as necessary and inevitable was shown to be contingent. The government realised that if it didn't defeat the challenge from the students, the whole project of austerity, marketisation and privatisation over the next five years would be called into question. As Nina Power argued, the movement didn't fail 'as much as it was deliberately crushed'.

## Uneven success

Not all British students 'lost' the vote on the raising of tuition fees. Only those in England were to be subject to higher fees. The experience of the student movements in Northern Ireland and Scotland highlights the misfortune of the English students.

In both Northern Ireland and Scotland, the tuition fees fight continued in the run-up to regional legislative elections in 2011. In both regions, the movement 'from below' of mass demonstrations was complemented by a lobbying strategy to convince politicians in the devolved assemblies. The lobbying strategy by NUS Scotland was so successful that only the Scottish Conservative Party said they would raise fees. Even Scottish Labour promised to keep them abolished, bucking the policy of £6,000 per year fees advocated by the national party. This was a major shift. On the 10th of November 2010, the SNP

Scottish Education Secretary Michael Russell said of tuition fees: 'I am not agreeing with that', but 'I'm not ruling it out.'[3] 'In Scotland it is the case that if it hadn't been for the protests [in London] and the amount of Scottish students who went to them, then I think the Scottish government might well have introduced them in Scotland', argued Gordon Maloney. Adam McGibbon, Vice President for Welfare at Queens University Belfast, agreed: 'the movement in England put students back on the agenda'. Alongside 'well-organised lobbying' and a successful 'demonstration in front of City Hall', a 'third crucial factor was that the Northern Ireland Assembly were terrified by what they saw in England – especially students getting kettled. There was the fear that something similar was going to happen to them ... The noise, the activism, and the occupations over in England created a credible space and political pressure' in the run up to Assembly election in May 2011.

The movements in Northern Ireland and Scotland show that the movement in London and English towns and cities was not in vain. They demonstrated the importance of combining a grassroots movement with a sympathetic national union that could lead and lobby. Furthermore, the experiences of the regions show how devolution provided greater openings for concentrated political lobbying unavailable to English students. Deputy President of the NUS-USI Lorcan Mullen noted the benefits of the 'consociational form of government which is particularly vulnerable to orchestrated forms of political lobbying', which the campaign in Northern Ireland pressured with 'some great protests and demonstrations, as well as a political strategy'. What felt like a crushing defeat for students in England laid the basis for successes elsewhere

– successes that students in Northern Ireland, Scotland and Wales are still struggling to defend.

## Movements from above and below

The key difference between the movement in England and those in Northern Ireland and Scotland was the relationship between the movement in the institutions and the movement in the streets – or the 'official' and 'unofficial' movements. In England, the strength of the movement in the street – mobilising at times hundreds of thousands of people – was unable to organise a successful strategy to win over lawmakers. The official student movement, represented by the NUS, was cut adrift from the spontaneous campaign that developed in the universities, colleges and demonstrations. The inability to combine the two was one of the movement's key weaknesses.

For participants, the lack of support from the NUS featured heavily. For Ben Beach, the obstacles to and the strengths of the movement were 'one and the same'. 'The key obstacle was the *total failure* of the NUS to provide any form of meaningful support. We had to figure it out as we went along.' 'The absolute cowardice' and 'treacherousness' of the NUS leadership, shown in the 'speed they took to condemn the student protesters' after Millbank, 'cannot be forgiven'. For Aadam Muuse, the NUS was failing school and college students by 'doing absolutely nothing on EMA disappearing. All their focus was on the tuition fee increase.' The campaign to save the EMA continued into January 2011, when a demonstration was organised without NUS support. 'The EMA battle could have been won. But by complete incompetence or wilful inaction – the NUS didn't mobilise to save EMA in the way they did over fees.'

The feeling of betrayal rested on an acknowledgement of the NUS's potential mobilising force, which the student organisations outside couldn't match. As Huw Lemmey noted: 'no demonstration was as big as the first NUS demonstration [on November 10th]. That is purely because NUS controls the buses.' The result was a fracture between the lobbying strategy conducted by NUS inside Parliament and the movement outside. For Michael Chessum, this divorce was 'paradoxical': 'We were using a street strategy to win a conventional lobbying vote. We were using a sledgehammer to crack a nut (and missing) … The NUS acted completely separately to us.'

Aaron Porter, the NUS President, became an intensely divisive figure for many involved in the protests. Alan Bailey, then the NUS LGBT Officer and an NEC member, remembers Porter pleading with him to try and calm the runaway protest movement: 'Alan, you have to stop them!' Yet while Michael Chessum rued the need for a 'few more men in suits who could walk up to men in Parliament', Porter and the NUS were doing exactly that. NUS officials and staffers extensively lobbied MPs on the day of the vote as they had done in the months before, focusing on 'wavering Conservatives like Justin Tomlinson and David Davis' and the 56 Liberal Democrat MPs. 'I think I met at least 40 of the 56 Lib-Dem MPs personally – some several times', Porter remembers. Liberal Democrat MPs, fearful of giving in to 'anguished students' and 'balaclava wearing, war-memorial tarnishing individuals', hampered the negotiations:

Liberal Democrat MPs told me that the ongoing nature of the protests made it less likely that they would change their position. That is an important thing that I understood and that others didn't … They actually thought, oddly, that showing they could stand up against public opinion would demonstrate themselves as a party that could hold power, and so get more power in the future. I got told by MPs who voted against – Charles Kennedy and Menzies Campbell – that 'we are going to vote against, but we are finding it hard to get our colleagues to vote with us because of the way the ongoing protests are transpiring'.

Porter was robustly challenged when he attended the UCL occupation on November 28th, apologising for being 'spineless and dithering'. He promised to provide 'financial, legal and political aid' and to call a demonstration on the day of the tuition fees vote.[4] Having previously called the protesters 'despicable', Porter was pressurised at the UCL occupation into offering them a message of support, even if he didn't agree with their overall strategy: 'Unfortunately [the occupiers] didn't quite appreciate that their strategy – to pressure the university management to put pressure on the Liberal Democrats – wouldn't work.' Vicki Baars, a member of the NUS National Executive Committee and NUS LGBT Officer, saw NUS control of the press contacts as a key weakness. 'Those of us on the left-wing of the NEC had very little control over press contacts and influence, meaning that the press coverage was always focused on the violence. That was a real weakness. The imagery all became about property damage and nothing else.'

How MPs reacted to the protests outside their offices highlights the problems in the movement's street strategy. Whereas students felt justified conducting this form of lobbying because of the Liberal Democrat's betrayal, MPs felt affronted that their everyday work had been forcibly disrupted. In Birmingham, a group of ten students occupied the office of the Liberal Democrat MP John Hemming. 'Clearly the students are not concerned about how their actions are affecting other people', Hemming said, after claiming his staff were prevented from doing constituency work. 'I have not made a formal decision as to how to vote on Thursday, but this sort of behaviour does not make me more inclined to support the case that they advocate.'⁵ Around 80 students protested outside Liberal Democrat MP Don Foster's constituency office. Foster confronted the students, telling them he would not make up his mind until a few hours before the vote. He eventually voted for the rise in fees. Within hours a stone had been thrown through the window of his constituency office, according to the *Bath Chronicle*.⁶ Students burnt an effigy of Nick Clegg outside the offices of *The Guardian* in Kings Cross, where he was giving the Hugo Young lecture.⁷

One of the first signals of the emerging movement came in Oxford, just before the Millbank demonstration. Nick Evans remembers 'people being taken back by the scale of it' with 'nearly 1,000 students' marching through the city on the 28th of October 2010, almost two weeks before Millbank. Organised by the group Oxford Education Campaign, the protest forced Vince Cable to pull out of a speaking engagement at the university. As Aaron Porter noted, the effect of the protests on MPs was limited. Cable could only 'vaguely' recall the Oxford demonstration: 'I vaguely remember the advice we got was that the mood was toxic and that all you would do if you went was add fuel to the fire. But I don't remember it very clearly, so it must not have been something significant.'

One major protest that Cable did remember, however, occurred at his constituency office in Twickenham, west

London, during his Friday evening surgery. This lobby of '50' students, (wrongly) believed by Cable to have been organised by the NUS, resulted in the infamous 'Cablegate' interview in which two undercover reporters encouraged the Business Secretary to let slip the extent of his opposition to Rupert Murdoch's influence over Britain's media.[8] Cable claimed that the protest didn't affect him at all:

> The NUS had a group who dispatched themselves to my constituency, and they were very, very, aggressive. Students had been drafted in from UCL … My staff were terrified – abused, shouted at, and jostled. There was aggressive banging on the door. That was when a journalist came along with a secret camera to get my thoughts on Murdoch. I was obviously quite churned up with all the screaming and banging. All my constituents had left and I then said more than I should have done. The Murdoch affair was much more traumatic politically and personally than the student protests … The protests didn't [affect me at all]. If anything, it was counterproductive. The people I tried to engage with were just so totally unreasonable and clearly not making any effort to understand the decision-making processes. If anything it hardened me.

Liberal Democrat MPs believed the NUS to be responsible for protests and occupations in which it had no part. The protest at Cable's constituency office was organised by the NCAFC and UCL occupiers, without NUS involvement. For Aaron Porter, this guilt-by-association was the 'worst of both worlds': 'We were implicated in protests that we didn't actually organise. It was a bit perverse that lots of students were very angry that NUS wasn't involved in the protests, but in the eyes of policy-makers we *were* involved organising them. It was the worst of both worlds.'

John Leech – then Liberal Democrat MP for Manchester Withington, rebel against the Coalition, and later unseated in the 2015 general election – saw the protests as at best inconsequential in affecting the attitudes of MPs, and at worst as having a negative effect:

I don't think they did [affect colleagues]. Because the people who voted against tuition fees were always going to vote against tuition fees. The way in which the really vicious and nasty campaign was waged against Liberal Democrat MPs in 2010 was far more likely to discourage people from voting against tuition fees. The manner in which it was done was pretty vile. I was always going to vote against tuition fees so there was nothing I could have done differently.

David Willetts agreed that elements of the protest were unproductive, but through interaction with protesters his perceptions of the EMA issue changed: 'In conversation, with a proper exchange of ideas, you can learn. I learnt how much the EMA issue really was upsetting people.' On the 22nd of November 2011 Willetts was 'shouted down' during a speech at Cambridge University by students protesting the marketisation of education. One PhD student, singled out by the university for leading the 'mic check' protest, was suspended from the university for seven terms (the decision was later rescinded). Willetts was advised not to attend universities for fear of protests. He remembers 'hairy' protests at SOAS and Bristol after 2010: 'It's very hard in a protest while you are being shouted at to change your mind ... I am not defensive about this policy. I believe it's the right thing to do.'

The division between the 'official' and 'unofficial' movements was one of the overarching themes of the protests. On the one hand, the 'official' movement was orientated towards lobbying MPs in Parliament through 'respectable' means. On the other hand, the movement outside felt betrayed by the whole political class. Young people were not in the mood for respectful back-room politics. Radical direct action was seen by activists as a logical response to Liberal Democrat's breaking of their electoral promise. This strength of feeling was not accounted for in the NUS's parliamentary strategy. The movement from below and the movement from above here came into glaring contradiction.

## Organisational brokers

The generation of 2010 would learn from their experiences. Many student activists made the 'long march through the institutions', advocated by German '68 veteran Rudi Dutschke, in the search of 2010's missing 'organisational broker'. Many later found themselves in leadership positions within the NUS. Uniting the movements from below and from above was made more difficult by the 'ideology of horizontals' pervading the movement. This 'horizontal' political sense matched a newly politicised generation of activists who had created a movement outside traditional party structures, lubricated by open access social media. For James Butler, it wasn't that the movement lacked leadership, but that a large section of the movement was not willing to have *any* leaders at all. For Butler, the influence of anti-hierarchical politics inherited from folk-anarchism and the climate movement played a large role in 'conceding the discursive and political territory to others'. 'You know: the inability to seize the moment because you 'don't have any leaders' and 'you don't have any spokespersons'. This was made harder, noted Aaron Bastani, by the dearth of organisational models to turn too: 'we didn't have the example of CLASSE in Quebec', which successfully conducted an indefinite student strike for over a year. 'After the ideological phase of the horizontals, no one recognised the need to go back to almost vertical "operation".'

The failure to find an organisational broker went further than the student movement. It was also a problem of political parties. In 2010, no political party could lay claim to be a leading 'voice of the movement'. While in Northern Ireland, as Lorcan Mullen noted, what was needed was to 'shore up support of the leading two parties to fulfil their pledges', in England the situation was more complicated. If an organisational broker was needed in Parliament to give support to the movement in the streets, leadership was not forthcoming from Ed Miliband. The ex-Labour leader thought about coming to the UCL occupation on the instigation of John Cruddas MP (who did attend), only to backtrack after a word from a press advisor.[9] Asked about the student occupations, Miliband said: 'I was quite tempted to go out and talk to them. I think I was doing something else at the time actually.' Asked if he would join future demonstrations, he responded: 'We'll see what happens.'[10] The Conservatives condemned Miliband's 'dithering'. For Mark Bergfeld, the problem was the lack of a meaningful 'political articulation', the lack of a sustained student strike, and the debilitating weight of historic political traditions. 'We didn't have a party in government or in

Parliament which was willing to stick its neck on the line and say: "we are the voice of this movement".

An overarching problem for all organisations active within the student movement was their inability to involve participants in their structures. The discrepancy between the numbers participating in the movement and those attending conferences hosted by EAN or NCAFC was striking. The same dynamic was also noted by Jamie Woodcock in the organisations formed to stop the Iraq War. The millions of protesters didn't correspond to the numbers joining either the Stop the War movement or the radical left groups that drove it organisationally. EAN was to dissolve itself in the coming years, while NCAFC continued to survive, though wracked by major disagreements.

The organisational broker didn't appear. Under the weight of past political traditions, British students, like the student militants of Nagisa Oshima's film *Night and Fog in Japan* (1960), were unable to break free from the past or right the failures of their organisations. The 2010 generation would have to wait years for changes in the NUS and the Labour Party.

## A question of strategy

While many of the problems were outside the control of the movement, some activists lamented its internal tactical and strategic failures. Ashok Kumar was more philosophical about the decline of the movement: 'You know, movements decline … Those who expect movements to continue indefinitely are not aware of the history of social movements or their dynamics.' 'We had countless demonstrations, petitions, and pressurised so many different people ... I don't know how much more you could have done', remarked Alexandra Chandran. For Ben Beach, on the other hand, a lot could have been done differently:

> I think one of the key failures was the inability to antagonise university managers enough to force them to come out against the bill they had all lobbied for ... We should have decommissioned their offices. We should have forced the demonstration of their files ... I think the occupations were too placid, aside from being organising bases. There's always a risk it can become 'radical camping'. In the end, we did just have a room in the university ... We could have had mobil-isations campus to campus, where one day everyone goes to SOAS, one day everyone goes to UCL ... There was never a time for deeper consideration, there was just open con-frontation.

This confrontational direct-action politics was hard to throw off as the movement declined. During the revolt, 'the way people were talking about direct action really did make it become an end in itself', remarked Matt Cole. An alternative to a self-defeating strategy of the 'propaganda of the deed' could be found in the 'community-organising perspective' advocated by Malia Bouattia. Becoming active in the NUS Black Students' campaign, and later NUS President, Bouattia saw a missed opportunity in failing to organise 'all these young further education and school kids that have come out in rebellion to resist this marketised future: what about them?'

In hindsight, activists noted a wide variety of strategic mistakes made by the movement. Memories cohere around the theme of unity and concentration: the failure to unite the movement from below and above; the failure to construct a lasting unity between school and university students; the failure to unite a political articulation in Parliament with a movement of the streets; and the failure to concentrate that unity at the key pressure points – university managements complicit in marketisation and the fissures running through the political class. The movement was over before the students could learn these lessons. Minerva's owl, as Hegel noted, flies only at dusk.

## Out of apathy?

Consecutive generations of the British New Left have taken the title of E.P. Thompson's edited volume *Out of Apathy* as a topic of serious concern.[11] Thompson's definition of apathy from the book's introduction has found few rivals. Apathy, he argues, is the state in which people look for *private* solutions to *public* evils. The passivity of British students, fostered by decades of neoliberalism, was one of the largest hurdles faced by the student revolt. It would take more than a month-long movement to shift deeply rooted popular conceptions and individualist patterns of behaviour, fostered by an ensemble of state instruments and market discipline.

The British student revolt was extraordinary because it emerged 'out of apathy'. Polls during the movement showed overwhelming opposition to the government plans, with 78 per cent of university students opposing the rise in tuition fees, while 80 per cent thought it was wrong for the Liberal Democrats to revoke their pledge.[12] Passive opposition, however, implies neither active resistance nor the triumph of collective endeavour over individual self-interest. Decades of political passivity on British campuses was a serious impediment to the movement. In 2000, Gary Younge had noted that campus indifference was not solely the result of a litany of NUS Presidents allied to the Labour Students faction (who closely followed the changing line of the Labour leadership), but was an 'inevitable corollary of the way in which campus life has changed over the past decade'. 'The student experience has become as fractured, variegated and disparate as the experience of work, retirement or childhood. Politics no longer dominates student culture because there is no such thing as "student culture"; Younge wrote.[13] Doug Rouxel, a lecturer at South Essex College in Southend, remembers his students being 'amazingly apathetic', having been completely 'integrated into management structures'. This tradition of disengagement had been fostered over the preceding decades.

The weight of student apathy, which researchers had been noting for decades, was matched by a more general disengagement of other social sectors. Malia Bouattia was struck by the negative public response to the student's cause: 'I remember while working part time at Costco going in on the weekend, and people just hating, saying: "I hope you aren't a part of it" ... [For them] this was just an act of terror, almost ... Instead of people seeing it as their struggle as well as the students' struggle it was just a total demonisation.' Members of the public interviewed at the November 10th NUS demonstration were also cynical. In Trafalgar Square an irate bus driver confessed: 'I was sympathetic until they blocked my bus.' A graphic designer from Devon, David, was even more judging: 'There is no such thing as free education. It is paid for by our taxes.'[14] David Willetts argued that 'there really wasn't that much sympathy for students': 'The images, Churchill's statue [defaced], to be honest eroded wider popular support for students – which is a pity as I am actually pro-student … It reinforced some people's perceptions of what students were like.'

Anecdotal evidence of public attitudes, however, is not an ideal measure of public opinion. A YouGov poll for *The Sunday Times* in November 2010 showed a clear majority of the population were against the government's plans on tuition fees – only 35 per cent supported the plans while 52 per cent opposed them. Asked about the Millbank protest, 65 per cent of people said they had some sympathy with the demonstration, while 13 per cent had sympathy with the direct action against the Conservative Party headquarters. Meanwhile 69 per cent thought the occupation had damaged the student's cause, with 11 per cent saying it had helped it; 87 per cent expected more violent protests against the coalition's cuts in future years.[15] Even if their opposition to the students might be contested, it is clear that few sections of the British public actively supported the students either on demonstrations or solidarity actions. The students were the first social sector to seriously mobilise against the policies of austerity, but they were left politically isolated with no party or organisation to represent them but themselves.

## Policing the crisis

The 2010 student revolt marked an important moment in the history of British policing. Not since the poll tax riots had such police repression been so openly displayed on British streets. Alfie Meadows, as discussed earlier, nearly died after being hit on the head by a police truncheon on December 9th. The police used horse charges, kettling, baton charges, pre-emptive raids of activists' houses under anti-terror legislation, and serially collected the contact details of lawful students. A total of 16 civil claims were made against the police by 100 claimants. Undeterred, the police pursued exemplary justice against offenders. Operation Malone was set up by the Scotland Yard to launch a 'major criminal investigation' into the protests for this end. Reviewing CCTV and police footage, the police made public appeals to identify alleged offenders. These resulted in the arrest of 175 people, including 34 from the December 9th demonstration. Natalie Graham saw the demobilising effect of the repression on her friends: 'for people who were new to the experience they just felt like "fuck this shit I'm going home"'. S.G. dropped out of activism after December 9th – demobilised by the vote passing and by the fear of recriminations by the police. 'It was the first time I actually took part in UK politics', S.G. recalled.

Some protesters were prepared for defeat, but others weren't. Charlotte Grace wasn't taken aback by the police violence: 'even when beaten badly on the first demonstration, I don't remember being shocked by it … I guess it was like some sort of rite of passage.' Alex Moore, from south London, had left school at 16 and was working as a day labourer during the 2010 protests. The police tactic of kettling put him off protesting. If the police wanted to dissuade young people from protesting in the future, they succeeded:

I didn't go to the later demonstrations after the November 24th demonstration in London, as by that point I hadn't got the sense that protesting was the way forward. Ever since

2010 and then in the 2011 London riots, it was the end of me ever wanting to protest again … 2010 deterred people from going against the government. It made things all very hopeless in my opinion.

The response by the police was not the only instrument of coercion the students faced. Their own universities and colleges, many implicated in formulating and lobbying for the reforms, used their legal and pastoral powers to clip the wings of the movement. Seeing the occupations as threats to their right to manage, the universities embarked on expensive legal action against their own students. Ben Beach describes how UCL attempted to evict the occupiers and the strategies the students used to combat it:

When we received the papers we decided to contest them in court … We basically set ourselves up in a bureaucratic fight that we had no hope of winning … The papers had been served by Eversheds, this company based in Manchester, and within four hours of them being served a bunch of comrades in Manchester had stormed their offices … Our lawyer was telling us to 'stop the strategy of escalation' and not to occupy anything else or do anything that might jeopardise the court case … At this point, UCL threatened costs against the students, effectively bankrupting us if we didn't stop … We should have forced them to evict us; we should have dared them to evict us and drag us out one by one.

Many school and college managements used a variety of instruments and threats to thwart the protesters. The financial recriminations against students on EMA, largely from poor and working-class backgrounds, was just another hurdle the movement had to jump. Aadam Muuse remembers the EMA issue being vital for college students: 'I don't think that level of sacrifice, potentially sacrificing your EMA, to go to the demonstrations was given as much platform in the public conversations.' Kieran Sutton remembers the 'threatening' and 'snide' attitude of his principal 'who threatened to cut students' EMA if they protested: "If you walk out of classroom you are not in attendance", the principal said. "You are marked 0 on register." That was really important for some people as if they miss one class a week then they would lose their EMA.' Unlike at Westminster Kingsway, all students at Aadam Muuse's school who wished to attend the November 24th demonstration would retain their EMA through an authorised absence. Muuse described the importance of the weekly grant for him and his peers:

Not having the EMA meant that some days you couldn't go to college. Some weeks when I didn't get EMA money it would be very difficult to do anything besides go to college and come home, as I was entitled to free school meals. Some people lived a tube ride away which meant you couldn't get to school. A friend of mine had to spend £25 on travel a week, which left him £5 for food for the whole week.

There were even greater barriers to organising walkouts at Shereen Prasad's school in Newham. There were multiple gates to pass through to enter the school, accessible only with the school's permission or a key card. To leave school would require a note from parents: 'For my school it was impossible to walkout. You couldn't even walkout as an individual let alone organise a mass walkout. Most people didn't even go to school let alone walkout. At a lot of the schools the security was just as tight as they had to worry about gang violence.'

College and school students, like those at university, could also take on the management of their institutions – even with the barriers put up to their participation. The threats by the principal at Westminster Kingsway spurred a protest on campus against him. Negotiations with the college's executive managers and local councillors were profoundly instructive for Kieran Sutton:

> The principal of the Westminster Kingsway called a meeting with local MPs and councillors. It was chaired by the Vice Principal – or some kind of college executive. On the panel were local Labour, Liberal Democrat and Tory councillors. That meeting changed my mind so clearly about the idea of 'the power of the argument versus the argument of power'. We were pleading with these people: 'please don't take away our EMA', 'please don't stop us going to university', 'please don't do this or that', and 'this is taking away our futures'. They just lied, shied away, or ignored it. There were 150 people there, in a big double room. That really changed my opinion about debating with people in power and fighting with people around you.

The repression of social movements can both spur renewed activity against perceived injustice and discourage future activity through increased risks. In the 2010 student revolt, repression was a powerful demobilising factor.

*Voting with your feet*

As Big Ben struck six on December 9th the protesting students would quickly learn that the government had prevailed. For those new to politics and with hopes bolstered by the movement, this was a critical check on their fledgling confidence. The failure was taken by many already wary of politics and parties as a vindication of their previous suspicions. Politics had never worked for them before, so why should the issue of tuition fees be any different? Kieran Sutton remembered 'my friends felt disappointment when the votes went through … A lot of us were getting over our previous naivety. It was a difficult time.' Shereen Prasad was standing in Parliament Square with her older brother when she heard the news:

I was like: 'No, that's not the way things are supposed to happen, that's not the way the world works. When people say no, it's supposed to be no.' In a really naive way I felt really confident – that this was something that we had to win. I remember going home to my dad and saying: 'I thought things were going to change', and he said 'this is the harsh world, they don't always listen to you'.

Having lost the vote, the activists that remained in the movement found it harder to mobilise students around them. Prasad remembers how 'losing the fight for education was a reason that people stopped listening to me when I was talking with my friends: "Didn't you fight for EMA and then didn't it go?", "Didn't you fight against tuition fees and didn't they do it anyway?", "What does fighting do?"' Although the 2011

London riots shared some of the student revolt's spirit, they were experienced entirely differently, as Prasad explained:

For them, the [2011 London] riots were so key because fighting meant ... actually getting something. 'Go on your little demonstrations', they would say to me. They knew that it didn't make any difference and the government didn't listen to them. 'This is how you get it done, you break things and people talk about you for days and days and days', they said. I couldn't argue against that, as it was kind of true ... People didn't stop talking about the riots for months. Whereas the student demos, a week later it was if they had never happened. The arguments I tried to have with them got harder as I got proved wrong, and eventually I couldn't argue with them about anything.

The [2011 London] riots were about saying: 'I am here and I exist ... You might not care that I exist; there are loads of police in my neighbourhood all the time; you are knocking down our football cage to build luxury flats that we are never going to afford to live in. I might end up in jail, dead, in a crap job, or selling drugs, but I exist. I matter.' The riots were about saying: 'something isn't right, you can't shoot us just because we are young black men. We aren't going to stand for it anymore.' That was the same sentiment in the student protests. We aren't going to stand being beaten down anymore: 'You have taken away our EMA and now you want to treble fees as well, you are about to bring in cuts that means my mum is about to lose benefit money ... It wasn't just Mark Duggan getting shot, it was about us being treated like shit.' The causes aren't related but the feeling and sentiment of both are almost exactly the same.

While peripheral activists dropped out completely, those more centrally involved became fatigued. As Alexandra Chandran noted, 'I think there are only so many demonstrations people can go on before they become jaded and say: "Where is this thing going?" It is very difficult to keep that momentum going.' 'After the fee vote, people said we wouldn't go away. But once people came back from holidays students freaked out and said, "fuck, I haven't done any work for the first term"', recounted Hannah Sketchley. 'Most of us had to put our studies on hold for a bit', remembered Naiara Bazin. 'I remember being like "oh god", I haven't done anything after coming back for the next term … We had given up our studies for a whole term and now people's priorities had shifted.' There were those who found it hard to adapt to the new circumstances. Many students were 'totally unprepared to deal with the end of the movement', recalls Jamie Woodcock. 'People were saying: "we can call another occupation and the movement will start again". Five people would call the occupation and four people would come. It became a personal failure of activists, not a political question.'

The decline in participation and momentum was made harder, Malia Bouattia remembers, because 'there were no alternative spaces in which to engage on the "what next?"… I guess the delusion set in.' 'The next year there was a whole new group of students who came in, expecting there to be a student movement', remembers Jamie Woodcock. Instead they found only embers from the fire last time.

The continuous and stringent examinations of the neoliberal university would act as another break on students' collective action. Gaining good grades in exams and finding a well-paid job would seem even more necessary as debts were set to rise. Jamie Woodcock remembers that he 'didn't go to a class for three months'. 'All we did was activism. We would get up in the morning make leaflets, print them, prepared in time for students arriving at college. We would leaflet all day talking to people, then organise actions on campus. It was non-stop all the time.' The manic, almost millenarian culture of 2010 would dissipate as quickly as it emerged.

*If the university is a factory, where are the workers?*

One major source of frustration for student activists at the time was the lack of practical support from academics and university workers. Since 1992 there have been an average of 100 to 250 strikes per year.[16] Strikes in British society have not just been low since the early 1990s, they have been consistently low. This applies to lecturers in higher education as much as to other sectors. Marking boycotts were organised by the lecturers' unions in 2006. Aimed to pressurise the government into using the new money from tuition fees to reverse the relative decline in academic pay, the boycott collapsed after the unions accepted a government offer, citing a breakdown in participation by lecturers. The NUS leadership was supportive of the action, but came under pressure from several student unions that campaigned against the boycott. When 2010 arrived, students remembered how isolated they felt in their struggle inside the university. As James Butler noted,

> it's really remarkable how curb-lined academics can be, you know … we tried everything to reach out to them. They all objected in private, but did nothing to publicise that fact … There are honourable exceptions, but you know …

anything for a quiet life. If they had been much more united and determined in their opposition we *could* have won.

Natalie Graham experienced a similar feeling at Leeds University: 'What I wonder now: where were the academics? Why didn't they go on strike? They did nothing.' There were barriers to academics and university workers that students didn't face. 'When people have mortgages and kids to worry about, then they're not necessarily going to be moving as quickly as the young youths, d'you know what I mean?' noted Gupt Singh. Activists in Manchester had more success in making links with workers in the city, and made it their key priority – even if this was largely a one-way relationship. Jamie Woodcock explains how socialist activists from the Manchester University occupation tried to 'spread the movement out into the different trade union branches in the city':

There was a stage where we did two meetings a day. We drew up an email list of every trade union branch in Manchester and just emailed everyone ... Many students who had never seen a picket line before, they met trade unionists for the first time. The exposure of each was important. Though seeing the trade unions doing nothing wasn't the most exciting thing in the world.

In some places teachers and lecturers did try and play an active role in the movement. Arianna Tassinari remembers that lecturers at SOAS 'were actually really supportive of the occupation ... I don't remember people being up in arms, as we weren't stopping lectures ... the vast majority of the school thought it was just normal SOAS.' In Cambridge, a group called the Cambridge Academic Campaign for Higher

Education (CACHE) published an open letter in support of the occupation. Priyamvada Gopal, a Cambridge academic and a leading force in CACHE, wrote in *The Guardian* of the 'real vandals … who inflict such violence through laws, budgets and the hypocritical language of shared pain feel entitled to demand non-violence'.[17] Goldsmiths lecturers were rebuked by the Prime Minister for their statement in solidarity with the Millbank demonstration: 'The real violence in this situation relates not to a smashed window but to the destructive impact of the cuts and privatisation', they said. The government condemned the lecturers as 'frankly irresponsible'.[18] In higher education some lecturers showed positive solidarity with the students, but this was largely a passive rather than active hand of friendship. Many students felt this wasn't enough.

Sometimes it was the lecturers who were more radical than the students. Douglas Rouxel, a lecturer at South Essex College, negotiated with his college management for two lecturers to go along and represent the UCU branch at the November 10th demonstration. While his own students were 'amazingly apathetic', Rouxel organised a speaker from one of the student occupations to address the Southend Trades Council during a pensions dispute in early 2011.

On a national level, Len McCluskey, as General Secretary of Unite the Union, vocally supported the students. The students had 'put the trade unions on the spot', he said.[19] The late Bob Crow, then General Secretary of the RMT union, attended the UCL occupation.[20] But such messages of solidarity or appearances at occupations were the limit of the slogan 'Students and Workers Unite and Fight'. The hopes that left-wing students had in the working class to carry on the fight started by the students failed to materialise. For Simon Hardy, 'the trade union leaders didn't do anything practical to help us, even if they did send messages of support'. 'For the 2010 generation to be told, after the fees vote, that they needed a movement that included the whole of society, and especially workers, was all rather academic', remembered Michael Chessum. A participant from the Goldsmiths occupation had proclaimed the university a factory which should be shut down. This university-factory failed to live to expectations. The students were left to fight alone.

*Conclusion*

British students faced challenges before, during and after the movement. While it is true that Scottish, Welsh and Northern Irish students escaped the fee rise, students in England did not. The mobilisations in the streets, universities and colleges failed to translate the creativity shown outside Parliament into political power inside. Although the movement was divided in front of the press and politicians – making an effective strategy very difficult – its tactics were not the main reason for the defeat. The problems were longstanding. Longstanding disengagement amongst students made organising an uphill struggle. The movement was handicapped by a historically demobilised student body, combined with a government ideologically, intellectually and politically committed to austerity. Extraordinary police repression made sure the 2010 generation would think again before protesting in the future. Although the student revolt focused on combating fees and cuts, the government's strategy wasn't conceived solely in relation to higher education. Had the students' demands been met it would have set a precedent for others affected by future rounds of austerity. To the disappointment of the students, the Coalition was not for turning.

# Conclusion

The student revolt was about more than higher tuition fees and education cuts. The reforms to education were intimately tied to the Coalition's wider strategy of austerity. The revolt marked a critical moment for the fledging government. Without passing its first test, British politics would have plunged again into uncertainty. The *Financial Times*, as the intellectual conscience of British business, understood this as much as the government. As a leader article in the newspaper argued:

> The student demonstrations represent the first direct and violent opposition [the government] has faced. And while the administration has come through undeflected – if perhaps shaken – it should learn some lessons ... Even if the student protests now fizzle out, they should be a reminder to the coalition of the need to prepare the public for coming changes, especially the austerity measures that will affect people's livelihoods ... The coalition may face wider opposition when state employees lose their jobs, public sector pensions are reduced and public services themselves are cut. This will affect many more people. The government now has a breathing space.[1]

Above all, 2010 was a *missed opportunity*. The student movement offered the first and most serious opportunity to break the Coalition's agenda of austerity before it had begun. As Gary Younge wrote on the day of the tuition fees vote, the threat the movement posed was 'much like the financial crisis bringing them on to the streets': 'contagion'. The government feared the students' 'energy, enthusiasm, militancy, rage and raucousness might burn in us all'.[2] But more than a missed opportunity to seriously challenge austerity, the student revolt was a missed opportunity to politicise a generation. Only a minority remained active after the defeat and the police repression. Journalists and politicians had for years lamented the disillusionment of young people with politics. Yet on seeing a mass youth movement full of creative energy emerging – like a many-headed hydra which it could not control – the government refused to listen. Like Yanis Varoufakis confronting    Eurogroup while Greek finance minister, it was if the students had not spoken'.[3] Instead the government retreated to familiar strategies of repression. Its wider priorities – austerity and self-preservation – overshadowed any concern for the well-being of Britain's kettled youth. The student revolt proved to young people that you could have a just cause, take to the streets, and nothing would happen. In fact, as the 2010 generation found out, things got worse, not better.

If the movement had won, its participants would have been spurred on to further activity. Kristin Ross argues that the importance of May 1968 lay in the political possibilities it opened up. For a brief moment, Ross writes, there was 'a shattering of social identities that allowed politics to take place'.[4] In '68, students and workers were able to escape from their preordained roles to create a new and radical egalitarianism. Like all truly mass movements, this coming together of hitherto distinct groups and the construction of new liberatory political subjects – across divides thought to be unbridgeable – was present also in the 2010 student revolt.

University students mixed with school students, working-class with middle-class youth, black with white, trade unionists with students. 'What I'm witnessing at Leeds', a journalist wrote of the city's occupation, 'is not a fragmentation, but an embryonic coagulation of disparate groups.'[5] School and college students, newly politicised university students and experienced student activists came together to create a tragically short-lived political subject. Mobilised against the EMA cuts, tripled tuition fees and wider social injustice, this new embryonic coalition was discovering what politics *could* mean.

It would be wrong, however, to frame the 2010 student movement as a total failure. For the 2010 generation, what seemed like a defeat may have laid the basis for future breakthroughs. The current Labour Party policy commitment to abolish tuition fees and restore college grants is the culmination of years of collective work by a whole generation of young people in Britain. Like in 2010, the June 2017 general election saw the 'graduate without a future' unite with young people from the 'slums of London' – this time to vote in their millions for a Corbyn-led Labour Party. Labour's 'free education' policy was initiated by two 2010 veterans: the current leader of the party, Jeremy Corbyn, and the shadow chancellor, John McDonnell. For the 2010 student rebels, William Morris's words from *A Dream of John Ball* seem fitting: 'I pondered all these things, and how men fight and lose the battle, and the thing that they fought for comes about in spite of their defeat, and when it comes turns out not to be what they meant, and other men have to fight for what they meant under another name.'[6] Without the 2010 student movement this break with Labour's past record would not have been possible.

*Punitive neoliberalism*

The government response to the student revolt encapsulates what William Davies has characterised 'punitive neoliberalism'.[7] The 'enemy within' of post-2008 neoliberalism is no longer the greedy and unproductive trade unionist, but the most vulnerable and the least able to resist. The 2010 student revolt exposed a neoliberalism that took its hegemony for granted. As the demonstration in Parliament Square showed, this hegemony rested less on argument than on force. The 2010 generation – facing police charges, kettles, batons, injunctions – confronted a government that had failed to convince the students whom the reforms were supposed to benefit.

The government, the police and the press – having become used to the quiet acquiescence of previously insurgent social groups – were caught unawares. The reforms were justified as being in the 'students' best interests'. Yet students didn't accept that government ministers knew their interests better than they did. The irony of a policy justified in the student interest arousing such a popular and spontaneous response was met with incredulity and condescension. 'The students don't know what they are protesting about', teachers said. 'They are misinformed … they don't know their own interests', said politicians. Unable to convince students that the government knew best, the reforms were imposed de facto. Vince Cable and David Willetts were proud of rather than apologetic for their policy. Both claimed that the protests didn't affect them, their decisions or their belief that they were acting in the interests of those kettled in the streets. Protesters and politicians seemed to exist in different worlds.

## Institutional afterlives

It is important not to overstate the movement's effect on British political life; nevertheless, its afterlives are tangible. The Liberal Democrats were weakened as a party. In May 2010, the party had polled at 45 per cent of the vote for university students, with the Conservatives on 21 per cent and Labour on 24 per cent.[8] At the end of November 2010, they were down to just 15 per cent.[9] At the 2015 elections they were decimated, going from 57 seats to just eight. In a final act of the 2010 student movement, Nick Clegg lost his seat of Sheffield Hallam in the 2017 general election. The words of former Liberal Democrat MP and tuition fee rebel Greg Mulholland on December 9th were not heeded: 'To Liberal Democrat colleagues who are listening to the argument and say that we need to get this issue out of the way and get the pain over with, I say, this will not finish with today's vote.'[10] Speaking nearly six years after his speech, Mulholland – who lost his seat of Leeds North West in the 2017 general election – echoes the same sentiment:

How could you not expect it [the electoral backlash in 2015]. It was that delusion and self-denial ... It was obvious what it would do. The arguments that were trotted out: 'oh well it could be a fairer system', 'you can tell people that you stuck to the second part of the pledge about voting for a fairer system'. It was pathetic to be honest – pathetic and dishonourable ... Considering the fact that we had put ourselves forward as a new fresh party, not tarnished by the usual broken promises of politics and politicians ... This was a hugely significant moment [for the Liberal Democrats], and in the short term it was disastrous.

Tim Farron, another Liberal Democrat rebel and future party leader, described the fees as 'the poll tax of our generation.'[11] There was a real precedent for Farron's claim. As rebel Tory MP Julian Lewis noted in a speech to a besieged Parliament, he and David Cameron had tried to 'sell the poll tax to the people' while employed as young Tory Party workers in the early 1990s: 'There were all sorts of elegant arguments to show that the poll tax was actually the best and the fairest policy … [yet] even if we have a policy that we genuinely think is fair, unless we can convince people that it truly is a fair policy, it will fail and be rejected.'[12]

David Cameron had learnt from the humiliating defeat of Thatcher's poll tax. Other leading Conservative Party figures cut their political teeth combating the students. At the time, Theresa May was Home Secretary, while Boris Johnson was Mayor of London. The student revolt was 'intolerable and all those involved will be pursued and … face the full force of the law', Johnson said.[13] The last Conservative cabinet minister before Theresa May to go from a face-off with a radical student movement to the post of Prime Minister was Margaret Thatcher.

Jeremy Corbyn and John McDonnell, who went on to become Leader of the Labour Party and Shadow Chancellor, were present on the protests and attended the university occupations. Both had close links with the 2010 generation and were the first points of contact for petitions of solidarity with arrested protesters. McDonnell and Corbyn were involved in the 2010 movement because they believed that true leadership meant immersing yourselves in the struggles of others. They faced the same risks as the protesters, as McDonnell showed when he faced down the police on the November 24th demonstration. The large majority of young people who voted for Corbyn's Labour and its programme at the 2017 general election is unsurprising given his past record.

Describing a new strategy for the German student movement after 1968, Rudi Dutschke coined the term 'the long march through the institutions'. Dutschke advocated that students enter institutions of civil and political society to transform both the institutions and themselves. Since 2010 a slowly but steadily increasing number of left-wing sabbatical officers were elected to the NUS and local student unions. The changes had a definite time-lag. Although a motion for a national demonstration was passed at the 2011 NUS conference, the political character of the organisation and its elected officials changed little. 'There wasn't a change in leadership in NUS, despite the fact that the NUS President had just sold us out', Malia Bouattia argued. Vicki Baars' election to a Vice President (Union Development) position in 2012 marked a 'turn of the tide' where more left-wing students and activists from the 2010 generation started to gain traction in the union. The breakthrough came at the NUS conference of April 2016 when Malia Bouattia was elected President. Alongside her was a new left-wing sabbatical team, all of whose activism can be traced back to the 2010 student movement. At the NUS's April 2017 conference, Bouattia failed to be re-elected as president.

In 2000 Gary Younge attended the NUS conference, complaining that 'if last week's National Union of Students annual conference is anything to go by, students are not even slightly repugnant, not even vaguely anti-social'. Younge continued: 'For the past decade and a half, Labour's student organisation has been not only running, but running down, the NUS to the point where it has been transformed from a mass campaigning organisation to little more than a provider of cheap booze and a crèche for would-be parliamentarians.'[14] As the Labour government instituted fees and top-up fees, so too the party's student wing shaped the NUS. 'Before 2010, the National Union of Students was dominated by Labour Students for nearly two decades', remembered Hareem Ghani. Under its leadership, the NUS failed to stop the 'abolition of universal grants, the erosion of mandatory grants, the end of housing and unemployment benefits and the introduction of loans.'[15] Yet after 2010, the Millbank generation had the final say. Aaron Porter, speaking before the 2017 NUS conference, saw the transformation:

> Unquestionably there is a relationship between the new NUS leadership and 2010 … The strategy – lobbying first, protest second – was overwhelmingly backed by conference [in 2010]. But what we have seen year on year since then has been an erosion of my position and my politics … I think there is a range of reasons for why that happened. I think the first one is that the strategy we took [in 2010] failed. So people can more legitimately say: 'we would have won'. I think we would have lost by more, but it does become plausible to say: 'we lost taking your route, let's take a different one'.

Jim Dickinson, a senior executive and manager in the NUS for many years, has seen the organisation change rapidly:

Certainly it has got a lot more cooler than it used to be to be radical, to go on demonstrations, to vehemently oppose issues, to be anti-capitalist, than 20 years ago. Certainly, when I was working there I would never be told by the [national full-time] officers – who I was effectively civil servant for – to prepare materials to encourage student unions to organise rent strikes. The shift to the left isn't as radical as made out, but its real.

Aadam Muuse, NUS Black Students' Officer, believes that 'if I hadn't had been involved before 2010, I wouldn't have been involved after'. Muuse, like other sabbatical officers, traces his political formation to the 2010 movement:

The issues of the most marginalised of students – black and other liberation groups – have become more important in the public conversations ... You have the bureaucracy of the movement trying to relate to those outside it, not just being a closed world of policy nerds and geeks. There is a definite ripple effect from 2010.

The political nature of the Labour Party and the NUS has for decades been interrelated. The change in the Labour Party leadership has made this more apparent. Jeremy Corbyn and John McDonnell have faced similar problems. NUS officials and activists confronted an institutional structure 'still in place from 2010', just as Corbyn and McDonnell inherited a largely unchanged Labour Party structure. As Malia Bouattia noted in January 2017:

I may be in this seat, as well as other officers, but it's still very much a machine that was designed to be as ineffective as it was in 2010. And that's part of the problem. You've got hundreds of people that are part of the organisation – that keep it going on any day to day basis – with a very set process and structure in place of how to do it ... It's still the same NUS, with a changed leadership.

Activists in the regions felt this tension as well. Gordon Maloney, who was a sabbatical officer at the University of Aberdeen student union and then President of NUS Scotland from 2013 to 2015, argues that the move of the 2010 activists into union structures may have been a misplaced strategy:

In both positions I wasn't able to do anything. The structures just aren't set up for stuff like supporting direct action, strikes, solidarity. I wonder if my time would have been better used ... organising ... The chat was: 'imagine if we could take over all the student unions, we would have all these resources behind us'. But what we started to find was that it was a burden – spending time in trustee meetings instead of door knocking, lecture shout-outs, leafleting.

I had a Skype chat with an organiser from CLASSE, the Quebec student union, just after I had got elected, telling him what the movement looked like here: that almost every union has paid sabbaticals, most have paid staff; that the NUS has a turnover of £60 million pounds annually, hundreds of staff members, and could round up thousands of people for campaigns. And this guy was like: 'you guys should be in charge of the whole country! We did what we did in Quebec with one full-time staff member' ... Over the last seven years, 2010 was the year we were the least organised and the least together, the least on the ball, and those demos were the biggest.

The NUS of Jim Dickinson and Aaron Porter's generation – the organisation which so disappointed activists in 2010 – was the spur for a new generation to become involved in its structures. Malia Bouattia continues:

[There was a] disbelief that an organisation that is supposed to be based on social justice, could undermine its supposed principles to such an extent … It defined all of us as [full-time NUS] officers, undoubtedly … The children of 2010, definitely … And [with] the scars of that. It left enough anger in us to continue. OK, apathy set in, and the disillusion and so on, but I kept the anger and the venom at the leadership that sold us out. I kept the images of Alfie Meadows in my head every single time I was in an NUS space, every time I ran for a position. I really thought I was going to walk away in 2010 … I guess we still chose to fight, because there was no other space in which to do so.

The 2010 student revolt, in its own small way, added momentum to the leftward shift in both the Labour Party and the NUS since 2010.

*Point zero*

The most compelling afterlives of the movement are not to be found in institutions, but on the level of personal subjectivity. The student revolt would decisively form the character of many of its participants. For Charlotte Grace, who grew up in a 'right-wing working-class family' from Birmingham, the movement was transformative: 'It's just a point in a line of history, but for me it's absolutely the beginning. It's point zero.' The movement was the starting point for a lifetime of political commitment:

> It gave me politics, so everything goes to that moment, for me. I try to go back to stuff before, given the intensely conservative Catholic upbringing I'd had, and sure I was resisting it and I did refuse to leave the playground against the Iraq War once, but I mean, I didn't have class consciousness or political articulation … So the way I see my entire life now – the way I see suffering and hardship – all sits within frameworks of class, the state, capital, etc. I've come a long way since that point too … [Yet] when I speak to people I realise that they don't have the same experience as me. I mean, I imagine naively that it was all so radicalising for people as if nothing happened before, but that's not true.

Kieran Sutton was also profoundly changed by his experiences in the movement. From growing up in Tottenham, with a political world-view which had been 'in the UKIP kind of direction', his politics were transformed by 'standing with people that I never thought I would stand with':

> Several of my friends in Tottenham were like 'it's all about race' – either black-nationalist or UKIP rightward-leaning people. It was all naive kind of stuff – still open to ideas and not really having a label. As a young teenager I hung out in Tottenham with predominantly white people, which doesn't

happen often. I shaved my hair off. I was continuously getting robbed by BME [Black and Minority Ethnic] people. It made you think: 'maybe it all is their fault'. You start to pick up the hype around immigration and blaming other people – blaming and scapegoating. 2010 fully changed that. I can't stress that enough ... Everyone had a goal. It was more about people being given a say. We hadn't been listened to all of our lives until everyone got involved. It was a life-changing experience for all of my friends and I ... It is an experience that changed me forever.

For Arnie Joahill, then a school student, 2010 was a political experience that fundamentally changed his life. It was almost a spiritual experience: 'I felt like I had been in an experience where the world would never be the same again. And really, for me, it never was. The movement wedded me to a political commitment to change the world, to organise. From that moment I couldn't go backwards.' Naiara Bazin experienced a similar change: '[2010] changed my life ... I have given up my studies and PhD to work for an organisation that facilitates student activism [People & Planet]. If I hadn't been there I wouldn't be here today. Some of my best friends from back then are still my best friends now. It was the beginning of my journey to develop myself politically.' Alexandra Chandran remembers how the movement 'changed me from someone who had vague ideals and principles to someone who was surer of her political views, which I still hold today'. 'It was life-changing for me', remembers James Butler. 'It involved things I'd been reading about that were happening before my eyes. That "electric feeling" I had never felt before.' The movement, although made collectively, was a profoundly personal experience.

On the twentieth anniversary of 1968, Paul Piccone argued for an 'unmasking' of some of the myths of '68, reproduced each decade by the memoirs of former activists.[16] Martin Klimke and Joachim Scharloth also stress the 'myth-making' hanging over 1968: 'in almost all European countries, the actual historical events have been transformed by subsequent narratives illustrating a vast array of nostalgia, condemnation, and myth-making'.[17] The profundity of the experience of the 2010 movement as 'year zero' for some participants makes 'over-romanticising' the student revolt an ever present problem. For Natalie Graham, activists from 2010 act as if 'Millbank was D-Day or something'. For some of her friends 'it was the moment when they got on board with politics *and* left politics … One of them went into fashion and the other works for an NGO charity. I don't talk about the movement and I haven't for years. But it's there for sure. I don't think you can forget it really … If Millbank was your first experience of politics!' Naiara Bazin had similar thoughts: 'Millbank generation? Um, yes? I guess a generation that had a lot of hope and energy and was completely politically crushed by the Tories … I remember at Millbank having an incredible sense of power – that we were making history … But if anything we have been crushed.' A mixture of nostalgia, myth-making and cynicism can be evoked by the same participant to describe 2010.

The most committed activists were the ones most affected by the movement. A study of 'non-participation' in the 2010 student movement, involving a survey of nearly 2,500 students from 22 universities, found that the movement mobilised less than a third of its supporters on university campuses.[18]

Two-thirds of non-participants 'broadly supported' the student protests, while only 22.3 per cent of correspondents said they actively participated. Only 5.8 per cent of students sided with the government over its tuition fee policy. The study concludes that the protests did leave residual effects amongst non-participants: 42.6 per cent of supportive non-participants said they were more politically engaged after the protests, while for those that did participate, 29.1 per cent made the same claim.[19] Even with this important study, participants were sceptical of a generational break. For Alan Bailey, 'there should be no over-romanticising [of the movement] ... People need to be honest and not overemphasise it.' Participants in the protests, at least subjectively, still had reservations about continuing levels of engagement. As Hannah Sketchley of UCL argued, the existence of a Millbank generation is open to debate:

Apart from activists who have stayed in the movement, I don't think the people on my course or those who popped into the occupation and came on the demonstrations would define themselves as a 'generation'. The movement was just something you did in the first year of university like everyone else. The movement did not necessarily have a lasting effect on absolutely everyone who was a casual participant, especially outside of London or big cities.

For many student activists today, the student revolt remains a cultural and political touchstone. For Malia Bouattia, there is a 'new generation that have heard about 2010, saw it on television, and have been politically organised under the 2010 generation – but also aware of the current state of things and what needs to be done, and are going to carry on doing it'. Even though she didn't participate directly, Hareem Ghani agrees: '2010 was a year that is remembered by student activists even today – predominantly because for many it marked the very beginning of the ongoing assault on our education.'

The notion of 'generations' doesn't produce unanimity amongst participants. Even so, the struggle's outcome does not devalue its significance, or the importance of the experience for its participants. As Frantz Fanon said: 'Each generation must, out of relative obscurity, discover its mission, fulfil it, or betray it.'[20] Out of obscurity the Millbank generation has set a marker for future student movements. Future generations can learn from its experiences.

### Consequences of the reforms

Far from having been resolved, the issues faced by the students in 2010 have only worsened. The highest tuition fees for under-graduate degrees in the industrialised world, extortionate accommodation costs, increasing interest on student debt, an unfriendly job market for graduates – all these figure in the minds of students. As Peter Scott has noted, what ministers really meant when they said they were 'putting students "at the heart of the system" (where they have always been) is that students are to be regarded almost exclusively as consumers who are purchasing their higher education.'[21] One of the great ironies of the reforms – aimed at creating a more cost-effective and efficient system – is that there may be no direct financial reward for government. Forecasts as early as 2014 suggested write-off costs stood at 45 per cent of every £10 billion loaned to students each year, meaning the Treasury would be set to 'get zero financial reward from the government's policy of tripling tuition fees'.[22] By 2042 this would leave £90 billion of the £200 billion loaned unpaid.[23] In 2010 the estimate of write-off costs was 28 per cent. This revaluation matches the worsening outlook for pay received by young adults and the oversupply of degrees in the labour market. As of August 2016 students from low-income families applying to university are no longer entitled to a maintenance grant for living costs and will have to take out an additional loan. One of the main 'achievements' of the Coalition was this 'progressive' measure of providing bursaries.[24] The reforms have failed even by the standards they set themselves.

The prospects for recent graduates are made worse not only by crippling debt, but also by an oversaturated labour market. A 2014 report found Britain had a higher rate of over-qualified workers than any OECD country other than Japan.[25] Poor students who borrow £53,000 at current rates will accrue interest of £282,420 if their student loan is left unpaid for the full 30 years.[26] In some subjects more than a quarter of graduates end up taking poorly paid jobs in retail, catering or bar work on graduating.[27] The Office for National Statistics calculated that in 2013, 47 per cent of graduates were in non-graduate jobs, up from 36 per cent in 2002. 'When I took over at UCAS in 2010', noted a representative, 'students chased places – now the places chase them.'[28] As numbers expand, the saturation of graduates in the labour market is set to become an increasing problem.

Students are no longer paying off their student loans or interest to the government but to private debt-holding companies. The Coalition first announced that it would seek to sell off the country's student debt in 2013.[29] George Osborne then declared that the terms of loans taken since 2012 could be varied retrospectively – a move that in the business world could attract sanctions or even prosecution. A letter written by one recent graduate to his MP, pointing out that his debt had increased by £800 in one year, went viral on the internet. Unaware that his interest would be compounded, he felt that he and others 'had been mis-sold the loan'.[30] Not only has the universities sector been opened up to market forces, but student debt has been privatised as well.

The Teaching Excellence Framework (TEF) was the latest in a long line of government policies intended to build on the reforms by the Coalition government. The TEF seeks to rank universities into categories of gold, silver and bronze based on their 'performance' for students, with the top ranked allowed to charge higher tuition fees. Nick Clegg had claimed in 2010 that the '£9,000 figure is only going to happen on an exceptional basis'.[31] In reality, fees across the board have been set at £9,000 and are now set to rise. The NUS called for a boycott of the TEF through an embargo on the National Student Survey – where students rate the performance of their universities each year. The bitter irony of the government's reforms is that the more a student likes an institution, the more students coming after them will pay.

Student satisfaction will depend on the quality of teaching. Yet the neoliberal university is now allotting more and more of the teaching load to casualised staff, who are often on poorly paid hourly contracts. More than 53 per cent of all academics in the UK manage on some form of insecure and non-permanent contract, while for junior academics the rate is around three quarters.[32] In 2015, while 70 per cent of the teaching staff at Birmingham University were on insecure contracts, the Vice Chancellor Sir David Eastwood received remuneration of £416,000.[33] This casualisation of staff, following the US model, will worsen teaching conditions as lecturers find it hard to reproduce long-term meaningful relationships with students.

Yet nowhere have conditions deteriorated so rapidly than in student housing. Universities are continuing to raise rents and privatise halls. Accommodation costs increased by 18 per cent between 2012–13 and 2015–16, with rents averaging £226 per week for London and £134 across the UK.[34] According to the NUS, over 50 per cent of students say they can't afford their basic expenses of rent and other bills.[35] In spring 2016, a thousand UCL students organised a rent strike, one of the largest in UK history. In protest at rat-infested halls and loud building work, they won rent freezes and a £350,000 accommodation bursary for disadvantaged students. One of the organisers explained their successful tactics: 'We knew that on the money side they could wait us out, but what they couldn't take was the damage to their image … We knew where the university's weak spots were.'[36] In words that echo some of the problems faced by the 2010 student revolt, an activist from the Radical Housing Network argues for new tactics: 'There's only so much you can do with demonstrations and marches … If you're actually withholding rent, it demonstrates how serious you are and it forces management to make a change.'[37] A series of occupations against 'profit-driven education' rocked LSE, UAL, King's College London and Goldsmiths in March 2015. Student activism didn't end after the student revolt of 2010, but has continued to flare up in new spheres and with new tactics.

*Shared subjectivities*

The Coalition government's higher education reforms swiftly transformed the whole student experience. Sustaining activism on campus has become harder as new hurdles to collective action have been created by the marketisation of courses, the closure of humanities departments, the cutting of the teaching grant, the disciplining of future debt and the rising interest on loans, inadequate provisions for student mental health, and the casualisation of lecturers' contracts and conditions. Rising rents, precarious work and low wages are experienced by the thousands of students trying to work and live through their degrees. The decision to take a degree now involves a cost-benefit calculation – a return on investment predicated on potential future earnings. Students are encouraged to become entrepreneurs investing in their own human capital. Taking a degree makes no economic sense if you earn less than you would have earned without one – what is called the 'graduate premium'. Students are now consumers of education at a price; institutions are the providers of the service; lecturers (including those on casualised contracts) are employed to facilitate the transaction through nurturing students' human capital. Students are encouraged to choose their university on the basis of which one will best increase their market potential.

The political implications of rising debt and marketisation have not been lost on student activists today. Hareem Ghani says that 'one of the biggest issues we have today is mobilising students to take action':

There is very much a defeatist attitude amongst the vast majority of the student body – especially the newer generation of students who have no idea of what university used to look like ... On the one hand, you have students who do have a very defeated and dispirited attitude, but on the other hand, you have a small minority who are keen to fight back against the government and against their universities because they want more from their university.

The fight against sexual harassment on campus, a key priority for Ghani as NUS Women's Officer, is being made harder: 'At a time when universities are acting like business models, their first priority is to protect a lecturer or professor and his or her income grant, as opposed to students who may have experienced sexual harassment or some form of misconduct from their lecturer.'

Malia Bouattia also recognises the huge barriers put up to student activists by the new education regime and by state policies towards minorities. One of these, the government's Prevent Strategy, has had a particularly damaging effect. Conceived by the government to combat terrorism, but severely criticised for restricting basic civil and religious freedoms, Prevent has made organising on campuses harder. Activists are finding it more difficult to register student societies, book rooms for meetings, and to agitate without fear of recrimination. This is adding further distractions that militate against political activity. All this considered, Bouattia notes, 'is it then any surprise that people don't necessarily want to go and attend their 6pm [activist meeting] on how to take on the state?'

The [real] student experience is the ability to question the world around you and to be critical of it, to be conscious, to engage in activities that you want to; whether it's artistic, whether it's creative, whether it's political, whatever. And there's less and less time to do that. There is the disappearance of student councils in student unions [democratic meetings open to all students], with less people engaging because they've got work ... Even small things like the constant battle with institutions to keep Wednesday afternoons free, or the attempt to create Saturday lectures. All these times in which you can otherwise be engaging are being clogged with something else. Furthermore, as the fees have increased, with the pressure of success, you are then also facing the bleakness of the job market ... it is unsurprising that students are thinking about picking subjects that are going to make them money.

## Concluding remarks

The lessons and spirit of 2010 are important to recover today. For its participants, the student revolt meant a feeling of collective power. The movement inspired the belief that collective action by young people could change things, that they would be listened to. Students showed how education could be free and liberated, outside market values. The occupations showed that education need not have a price tag, and that space on campus was what students made of it. The 2010 generation showed that students constitute a moral and democratic force in society, that young people can act as the upholders of political virtues and democratic pledges – that they could represent the conscience of the nation. They also showed that students could defend their obligations to future generations, rather than thinking only for themselves, and that young people could create a force that unified, enthused and included those who had hitherto felt *outside* politics.

For the 'children of 2010' the solution is not to mourn, but to organise.

The 2010 student revolt is made of a patchwork of interlaced narratives and individual stories. The movement was both ultramodern and forward thinking, yet also bore the heavy weight of history. It played host to innovatory tactics and experiments with social media, as well as political methods with long pedigrees. It was a point of concentration – a contradictory overlapping of networks – each testing the other in the quickened atmosphere produced by the mass movement. A revolt by previously disorganised people shook the British state, but was dispersed almost as soon as it had begun. It was a moment of heightened transition, a catalyst in the decomposition of old politics and organisations and the founding of new experiences and new methods of organising – even if its organisational forms proved transitory.

The student revolt was important sociologically and politically. 'From Millbank to the summer riots – the scale of British discontent looks small beside the Arab Spring', noted Paul Mason, 'it's been possible to ignore its significance.'[38] But given how few serious challenges have been made in Britain to the politics of neoliberalism and austerity, each movement which does is all the more precious. The 2010 movement was defeated, and its significance should not be overplayed. Yet after any movement declines and fades from conscious memory one can say: 'was it ever that important?', 'was it ever that deeply rooted?', 'was it not so ephemeral as to be of no consequence?' Historians, as well as participants, have attempted to dethrone the experience of May 1968.

The historian François Furet announced that 'the French Revolution is over' as the movements of the late 1960s stalled.[39] 'Forget 68', declared one-time student leader Daniel Cohn-Bendit.[40] Yet whenever any new student movement emerges, a barrage of comparisons to 1968 results. There is good reason for this. In these brief transgressive outbreaks, glimpses of other ways of living and interacting can be seen. They are moments where the rulers sleep uneasily and where those barred from the political process take control. That is why the historical comparison continues to have traction in the popular imagination. Any future student movement in Britain cannot help but be compared to 2010.

It has not been this book's aim to wallow in nostalgia. Following the French socialist Jean Jaurès, tradition should not be viewed as the worship of ashes, but as the preservation of fire.[41] The feeling of collective power experienced by those involved in the 2010 protests is not devalued because it was ephemeral. The revolt's significance is all the more real because it seems so at odds with the current order of things. Passing on the flame is necessary, above all, to convince future generations that another world is possible.

# *List of Contributors*

*The date of interview is given in brackets*

A. (21/09/16) was a school student from south London, who wished to remain anonymous.

*Aadam Muuse* (19/09/16) attended Sir John Cass Sixth Form College in Tower Hamlets, East London, during 2010. He went on to become NUS Black Students' Officer 2016–17.

*Aaron Bastani* (23/10/15) was a PhD student at Royal Holloway University in 2010. He was a participant in the UCL occupation and a founder of Novara Media.

*Aaron Porter* (19/09/16) was President of the National Union of Students (2010–11).

*Adam McGibbon* (15/10/15) had just been elected Vice President of the Queen's University Students' Union in 2010. He would go on to work for the Green Party, running Caroline Lucas MP's 2015 re-election campaign.

*Alan Bailey* (15/10/15) was the NUS LGBT Officer in 2010 now works as a staff member in a students' union.

*Alex Moore* (06/09/16) was a labourer in 2010 and had left school before the start of the protests. He lives in south London.

*Alexandra Chandran* (11/12/15) was a student at Queen Mary, University of London studying International Relations. She now works for a Tech company.

*Arianna Tassinari* (31/10/15) was a third-year undergraduate student at SOAS in 2010. She now studies for a PhD in Industrial Relations at the University of Warwick.

*Arnie Joahill* (09/12/15) was a school student at Chiswick Community School in 2010. He is a black and Asian community organiser and graduated from the University of East London.

*Ashok Kumar* (06/10/15) was the Education Officer of LSE students' union in 2010–11. He is currently part of the Geography Faculty at Queen Mary, University of London.

*Barnaby Raine* (28/01/16) was 15 in 2010. He is now a PhD student in History at Columbia University.

*Ben Beach* (08/10/15) was an architecture student at UCL in 2010. He now works as a junior architect and is involved with the Radical Housing Network's Rent Strike Working Group.

*Charlotte Grace* (25/01/16) was finishing an architecture degree in 2010. She lives in London and is involved with Concrete Action and Novara Media.

*Clare Solomon* (25/10/15) was the President of the University of London Union in 2010.

*Craig Gent* (20/10/15) was a university student at Royal Holloway, University of London in 2010. He is now a senior editor at Novara Media, workplace organiser and PhD candidate.

*David Willetts* (31/01/17) was Minister of State for Universities and Science in 2010 and Conservative MP for Havant. He is now Executive Chair of the Resolution Foundation.

*Doug Rouxel* (19/10/15) was a lecturer and branch secretary of his UCU branch at a large further education college in Essex in 2010. He is currently a lecturer and chair of his UCU branch at a University in the Midlands.

*Ed McNally* (28/02/16) was 13 in 2010 and took part in a walkout from Chorton High School in Manchester. He is now an under-graduate at Cambridge University.

*Ed Maltby* (28/02/15) is a translator and a Marxist. He lives in North London and was a founder of the National Campaign Against Fees and Cuts.

*Gordon Maloney* (05/01/17) was a student at Aberdeen University in 2010. He went on to be elected as President of NUS Scotland, and currently works as a campaigner for 38 Degrees.

*Greg Mulholland* (19/10/16) was the Liberal Democrat MP for Leeds North West. He kept his promise to vote against any rise in tuition fees. He lost his seat at the June 2017 general election to the Labour Party.

*Gupt Singh* (25/11/15) was unemployed in 2010 and a full-time activist for a socialist organisation.

*Hannah Sketchley* (16/09/15) was in her first year at UCL in 2010, studying German and History. She became a sabbatical officer at UCL Union and continues to work in student unions.

*Hareem Ghani* (27/1/17) was NUS Women's Officer 2016–17 and a school student in South West London during the 2010 protests.

*Huw Lemmey* (27/02/16) worked in maintenance at Goldsmiths, University of London in 2011. He is now a writer and editor.

*Jacob Bard-Rosenberg* (28/01/16) was active organising students and workers in Bloomsbury in 2010.

*Jamie Woodcock* (09/12/15) was a student at the University of Manchester at the time and an activist in the SWP. He is now a Fellow at the LSE doing research on precarious work and digital labour, and no longer in the SWP.

*James Butler* (19/10/15) is a senior editor at *Novara Media*.

*Jim Dickinson* (06/01/17) was the Director of Campaigns and Policy at the National Union of Students in 2010.

*Joana Ramiro* (23/10/15) was the chief press officer and one of the co-founders of the National Campaign Against Fees and Cuts. She is now a journalist.

*Joe Ryle* (29/12/15) was a student at Leeds University and was active in the climate movement in 2010.

*John Leech* (10/10/16) was Liberal Democrat MP for Manchester Withington in 2010. He kept his pledge to vote against any rise in tuition fees. He lost his parliamentary seat at the 2015 general election.

*Kanja Sesay* (14/01/17) was NUS Black Students' Officer in 2010. He now works for Oxford Brookes University as an Equality, Diversity and Inclusion Adviser.

*Kieran Sutton* (09/09/16) was a student at Westminster Kingsway College in central London. He lives in London.

*Koshka Duff* (01/03/16) was a postgraduate student at Birkbeck in 2010 and now teaches philosophy at Kings College London.

*Lorcan Mullen* (19/10/15) studied law at Queen's University Belfast and served as NUS-USI Deputy President during the 2010–11 protests. He is now a trade union organiser with UNISON in North East Scotland.

*Luke Cooper* (20/10/15) was a PhD student at Sussex University in 2010. He is now a senior lecturer in Politics at Anglia Ruskin University.

*Malia Bouattia* (03/01/17) was a Masters student at the University of Birmingham in 2010. After two years as Black Students' Officer she was elected the NUS President at its April 2016 conference.

*Mark Bergfeld* (30/10/15) was former NEC member of the NUS (2010–12) and active with the Education Activist Network. He is a labour scholar and trade union consultant.

*Matt Cole* (01/03/16) was a postgraduate student at Kingston University from 2010–11. He is currently a PhD candidate at the University of Leeds, researching the political economy of hospitality work in the UK.

*Michael Chessum* (15/09/15) was a sabbatical officer at UCL student union in 2010, going on to become the President of ULU until it was closed in 2013.

*Naiara Bazin* (16/01/17) was a Biology student at Cambridge University and now works for People & Planet as part of the Movement Building team.

*Natalie Graham* (27/11/15) was a first-year English Literature student at Leeds University during the 2010 protests, she continues to be politically active.

*Nick Evans* (16/09/15) was an undergraduate studying History and Russian at Oxford University in 2010, and a socialist activist. He is still engaged in full-time historical research.

*Nina Power* (07/01/6) taught Philosophy at the University of Roehampton in 2010. She now teaches Critical Writing in Art and Design at the Royal College of Art.

*Ruth* (14/10/15) was a PhD student at the University of Warwick in 2010. She is currently working as an academic in her chosen field.

*S.G.* (31/10/15) was a Sociology and Media Production student at the University of Brighton in 2010. They grew up in east London.

*Sai Englert* (24/10/15) is a PhD candidate at SOAS University. In 2010, he was a Masters student at Sussex University and a member of the Education Activist Network.

*Sean Rillo-Raczka* (14/10/15) was chair of Birkbeck Student Union in 2010. He lives in east London.

*Shereen Prasad* (01/12/15) was 15 in 2010 and a school student at the Little Ilford School in Newham. She is now training to be a nurse.

*Simon Hardy* (14/10/15) was a founding member of the NCAFC. He lives in south London.

*Vicki Baars* (08/03/16) was NUS LGBT Officer in 2010. She would later be elected as NUS Vice President (Union Development) in 2012. She works in Equality, Diversity and Inclusion in Higher Education.

*Vince Cable* (16/09/16) is Liberal Democrat MP for Twickenham. He was Secretary of State for Business, Innovation and Skills in 2010. He lost his parliamentary seat at the 2015 general election but regained it at the June 2017 election.

*Will D.* (18/10/15) was a school student in Buckingham in 2010. He now lives and works in London.

*Will Searby* (02/12/15) was active in the Woodcraft Folk during the 2010 student movement and is now a postgraduate student.

# Notes

*1 Revolt*

1. Jean-Paul Sartre, 'Classe e partito', *Il Manifesto*, No. 4, 1 September 1969. 'The field of the possible is much vaster than the dominant classes have accustomed us to believing.'
2. *Financial Times*, 11 December 2010.
3. *Guardian*, 11 December 2010.
4. Manuel Castells, *Networks of Outrage and Hope: Social Movements in the Internet* Age (London: Polity, 2012), p. 222.
5. Rémy Herrera, 'Three Moments of the French Revolt', *Monthly Review*, 58:2 (2006).
6. Paul Mason, *Why It's Kicking Off Everywhere: The New Global Revolutions* (London: Verso, 2012), p. 45.
7. Tariq Ali, 'The Stories Continue …', *Guardian: G2*, 27 December 2010.
8. All unreferenced quotations in the book are from interviews with the participants.
9. Stuart Fox, *Apathy, Alienation and Young People: The Political Engagement of British Millennials*, PhD thesis, University of Nottingham, 2015.
10. 'Nick Clegg Urges Students to See "True Picture" on Fees', BBC News, 30 November 2010, http://www.bbc.co.uk/news/uk-politics-11870818.
11. David Cameron, Prime Minister's Speech on Education, 8 December 2010, Cabinet Office, CentreForum, https://www.gov.uk/government/speeches/pms-speech-on-education.
12. *Evening Standard*, 9 December 2010.
13. Cameron, Prime Minister's Speech on Education, 8 December 2010.

14. Hansard, Public Order Policing, 13 December 2010, Volume 520.

15. Ibid.

16. Polly Toynbee, 'Sorry, Students, But You're Low Down in the Pain Pecking Order', *Guardian*, 5 November 2010.

17. Jan Moir, 'Not so Jolly Hockey Sticks at the St Trinian's Riots', *Daily Mail*, 26 November 2010.

18. *The Times*, 11 November 2010.

19. Deborah Orr, 'Protesting Against the Cuts is Pointless', *Guardian*, 2 December 2010.

20. *Guardian*, 11 December 2010; Hansard, Public Order Policing, Duncan Hames (Lib), 13 December 2010, Volume 520.

21. E.P. Thompson, *The Making of the English Working Class* (New York: Vintage Books, 1966), p. 68.

22. E.P. Thompson, 'The Moral Economy of the English Crowd in the 18th Century', *Past & Present*, 50 (February 1971), pp. 76–136.

23. Mark Fisher, *Capitalist Realism* (London: Zero Books, 2009).

24. Mark Fisher, 'WINTER OF DISCONTENT 2.0: NOTES ON A MONTH OF MILITANCY', k-punk blog, 13 December 2010, http://k-punk.abstractdynamics.org/archives/2010_12.html.

25. Alan Travis and Caelainn Barr, '"Youthquake" Behind Labour Election Surge Divides Generations', *The Guardian*, 20 June 2017.

26. Lord Browne, *An Independent Review of Higher Education Funding and Student Finance in England*, 12 October 2010, National Archives (UK).

27. OECD, Education at a Glance 2015, 24 November 2015, http://www.oecd-ilibrary.org.

28. Department for Business, Innovation and Skills, *Putting Students at the Heart of the System*, Higher Education Report, June 2011.

29. Stefan Collini, 'Browne's Gamble', *London Review of Books*, 4 November 2010.

30. David Willetts, 'Oral Statement to Parliament, Universities UK Spring Conference 2011', 25 February 2011.

31. Liberal Democrat Manifesto 2010, p. 33.
32. Liberal Democrat Manifesto 2010, p. 39.
33. Paul Whiteley, *The Student Vote in 2010*, Opinion Panel Research, http://www.opinionpanel.co.uk/clientUpload/pdf/TheStudentVote2010.pdf.
34. *Guardian*, 14 November 1984; *Guardian*, 28 November 1984.
35. Dearing Report, *Higher Education in the Learning Society* (London: HMSO, 1997).
36. Ibid.
37. Denis Lawton, *Education and Labour Party Ideologies 1900–2001 and Beyond* (London: Routledge, 2005).
38. Ibid.
39. Gary Younge, 'Students Are Not Revolting: British Campus Culture is Dead, and Along With it Has Gone the Last Vestiges of Militancy', *Guardian*, 10 April 2000.
40. *Guardian*, 28 April 1998.
41. *Guardian*, 19 January 1999.
42. *Independent*, 16 November 2000.
43. *Independent*, 16 November 2000.
44. *Guardian*, 14 November 2000.
45. *Guardian*, 5 March 1998.
46. '"No Free Lunch", Students Told', BBC News, 15 November 2002, http://news.bbc.co.uk/1/hi/education/2479919.stm.
47. *Guardian*, 22 January 2003.
48. Benjamin Giguere and Richard Lalande, 'Why Do Students Strike? Direct and Indirect Determinants of Collective Action Participation', *Political Psychology*, 31 (2010), pp. 227–47.
49. Michael Gross, 'Bologna Resistance', *Current Biology*, 20:2 (2010).
50. *Guardian*, 16 December 2003.
51. *Guardian*, 27 October 2003.
52. *Guardian*, 27 October 2003.
53. 'Tuition Fees Timeline', BBC News, 16 March 2009, http://news.bbc.co.uk/1/hi/education/7923093.stm.
54. 'Students Drop Opposition to Fees', BBC News, 4 April 2008, http://news.bbc.co.uk/1/hi/education/7330231.stm.

55. OECD, Education at a Glance 2015, 24 November 2015, Table B3.2b, http://www.oecd-ilibrary.org.

56. Ibid.

57. Gerard Degroot (ed.), *Student Protest: The Sixties and After* (London: Routledge, 1998), pp. 54–9.

58. Ibid., pp. 66–7.

59. Hunt Janin, *The University in Medieval Life, 1179–1499* (Jefferson, NC: McFarland and Company, 2008).

60. Ibid.

61. Eric Ashby and Mary Anderson, *The Rise of the Student Estate in Britain* (London: Macmillan and Co Ltd, 1970).

62. Georgina Brewis, *A Social History of Student Volunteering: Britain and Beyond, 1880–1980* (Basingstoke: Palgrave Macmillan, 2014), Chapter 5.

63. Brian Simon, 'The Student Movement in England and Wales During the 1930s', *History of Education*, 16:3 (1987), pp. 189–203.

64. Richard Aldrich (ed.), *A Century of Education* (London: Routledge, 2002), p. 81.

65. Roy Lowe, 'The Expansion of Higher Education in England', in K. Jarausche (ed.), *The Transformation of Higher Learning, 1860–1930* (Chicago: Chicago University Press, 1982), pp. 37–56.

66. Quoted in R. Benn and R. Fieldhouse, 'Government Policies on University Expansion and Wider Access, 1945–51 and 1985–91 Compared', *Studies in Higher Education*, 18:3 (2003), pp. 299–313.

67. Aldrich (ed.), *A Century of Education*, p. 85.

68. E.P. Thompson (ed.), *Warwick University Ltd* (London: Spokesman Books, 1970).

69. Gareth Steadman Jones, 'Student Power: Problems, Diagnosis, Action', in Alexander Cockburn and Robin Blackburn (eds), *Student Power* (Harmondsworth: Penguin Books, 1969), p. 45.

70. Sian Anderson, 'Don't Blame us For Political Apathy', *Guardian*, 4 March 2010; Rodney Barker, 'The Lost Voice of Protest', *Guardian*, 25 September 2001.

71. Jonathan Jones, 'The Riot Girls', *Guardian*, 26 November 2010.

72. Polly Toynbee, 'Thatcher's Children Can Lead the Class of 68 Back Into Action', *Guardian*, 27 November 2010.

73. Brian Groom, 'Protests With Style, But a Bum Note', *Financial Times*, 7 December 2010.

74. Jonathan Guthrie, 'Shallow Radicalism of Tuition Sedition', *Financial Times*, 10 December 2010.

75. Laurie Penny, 'Out with the Old Politics', *Guardian*, 24 December 2010.

76. Alessandro Portelli, *The Battle of Valle Giulia: Oral History and the Art of Dialogue* (Wisconsin: University of Wisconsin Press, 1997), p. 184.

77. Ibid., p. xii.

78. Ibid., p. 12.

79. Luisa Passerini, *Autobiography of a Generation* (Middletown, CT: Wesleyan University Press, 1996), p. 1.

80. In Ronald Grele (ed.), *Envelopes of Sound: The Art of Oral History* (Chicago: Precedent Publishing, 1975), p. 75.

81. Dan Hancox (ed.), *Fight Back! A Reader on the Winter of Protest* (London: Open Democracy, 2011); Clare Solomon and Tania Palmieri (eds), *Springtime: The New Student Rebellions* (London: Verso, 2011); Michael Bailey and Des Freedman (eds), *The Assault on Universities: A Manifesto of Resistance* (London: Pluto, 2011).

82. Ronald Fraser, *1968: A Student Generation in Revolt* (London: Pantheon Books, 1988), p. 6.

83. Passerini, *Autobiography of a Generation*, p. 1.

84. Raphael Samuel, 'Perils of Transcript', *Oral History*, 1:2 (1971), pp. 19–22.

85. Eric Hobsbawm, *On History* (London: Abacus, 1999), p. 206.

86. Paul Thompson, *Voice of the Past* (Oxford: Oxford University Press, 1979), p. 64.

87. Fraser, *1968: A Student Generation in Revolt*, p. 5.

88. Luisa Passerini, 'Work Ideology and Consensus Under Italian Fascism', *History Workshop*, 8 (Autumn 1979), pp. 82–108.

89. Portelli, *The Battle of Valle Giulia*, p. xiv.

90. Thompson, *Voice of the Past*, p. 226.

91. Shiv Malik, *The Jilted Generation* (London: Icon Books, 2010); Hancox (ed.), *Fight Back! A Reader on the Winter of Protest*; David Willetts, *The Pinch: How the Baby Boomers Took Their Children's Future – And Why They Should Give it Back* (London: Atlantic, 2011).

92. *Karl Mannheim: Essays on the Sociology of Knowledge* (London: Routledge & Kegan Paul, 1972), p. 291.

93. In Cockburn and Blackburn (eds), *Student Power*, p. 28.

94. Walter Benjamin, 'Excavation and Memory' (1932), in *Selected Writings, Vol. 2, Part 2 (1931–1934)* (Cambridge, MA: Harvard University Press, 2005), p. 576.

## 2   Millbank

1. *Morning Star*, 12 November 2010.

2. Mason, *Why It's Kicking Off Everywhere*, p. 43.

3. *The Times*, 11 November 2010.

4. *Guardian*, 11 November 2010.

5. *The Times*, 11 November 2010.

6. *Guardian*, 11 November 2010.

7. *The Times*, 11 November 2010.

8. *Irish Times*, 4 November 2010.

9. *The Times*, 11 November 2010.

10. Ibid.

11. Ibid.

12. Ibid.

13. *The Sun*, 11 November 2010.

14. *Guardian*, 4 March 1968.

15. *The Times*, 8 May 1968.

16. Joanna Biggs, 'At the Occupation', *London Review of Books*, 16 December 2010.

17. Edward Woollard later handed himself in to the police on the advice of his mother.

18. Solomon and Palmieri (eds), *Springtime: The New Student Rebellions*, p. 76.

## 3  Expectations

1. Laurie Penny, 'Inside the Millbank Tower', *New Statesman*, 11 November 2010.
2. *The Times*, 11 November 2010.
3. *Guardian*, 26 November 2010.
4. *Guardian*, 11 November 2010.
5. Peter Mair, *Ruling the Void: The Hollowing of Western Democracy* (London: Verso, 2013), p. 23.
6. *Guardian*, 12 November 2010.
7. Ibid.
8. Ibid.
9. Anthony Barnett, 'Student Power: 1968 ... 2010', *Open Democracy*, 27 November 2010.
10. Fraser, *1968: A Student Generation in Revolt*, p. 244.
11. Ibid. Quotation from Pete Gowan, a Birmingham University student.

## 4  Street Fighting Youth

1. John Berger, 'The Nature of Mass Demonstrations', *New Society*, 23 May 1968.
2. Ibid.
3. Rosa Luxemburg, *Reform or Revolution* and *The Mass Strike* (Chicago: Haymarket, 2008), p. 140.
4. *The Times*, 25 November 2010.
5. *Guardian*, 27 November 2010.
6. *The Times*, 25 November 2010.
7. *Guardian*, 27 November 2010.
8. *Guardian*, 26 November 2010.
9. *Financial Times*, 25 November 2010.
10. *Guardian*, 27 November 2010.
11. Ibid.
12. *Guardian*, 24 November 2010.
13. *Liverpool Echo*, 22 November 2010.
14. Ibid.

15. *Bath Chronicle*, 25 November 2010.

16. *Burnley Express*, 25 November 2010.

17. Ibid.

18. *Yorkshire Post*, 25 November 2010.

19. Steve Cunningham and Michael Lavalette, *Schools Out! The Hidden History of Britain's School Student Strikes* (London: Bookmarks, 2016), p. 33.

20. Hansard, Public Order Policing, Christopher Pincher (Cons), 13 December 2010, Volume 520.

21. *Oxford Mail*, 1 December 2010.

22. Ibid.

23. *Exeter Express and Echo*, 2 December 2010.

24. Colin Barker, 'Some Reflections on Student Movements of the 1960s and Early 1970s', *Revista Crítica de Ciências Sociais*, 81 (2008), pp. 43–91.

25. *Financial Times*, 17 December 2010.

26. *Guardian*, 10 December 2010.

27. Hansard, Higher Education Fees, Jeremy Corbyn (Lab), 9 December 2010, Volume 520.

28. *Guardian*, 7 December 2010.

29. BBC *Newsnight*, 9 December 2010.

30. Ibid.

31. Mark Fisher, 'WINTER OF DISCONTENT 2.0: NOTES ON A MONTH OF MILITANCY', k-punk blog, 13 December 2010.

32. Lethal Bizzle – Pow – Rave in Parliament Square, London – Anti Cuts Protest X3 – 09/12/10, https://www.youtube.com/watch?v=WFDobI7CqNA.

33. *Guardian*, 4 November 2011.

34. Tempa T quoted in Dan Hancox, 'Pow!: An Anthem for Kettled Youth', *Guardian*, 3 February 2011.

35. *The Times*, 10 December 2010.

36. Hansard, Public Order Policing, Theresa May, Secretary of State for the Home Department, 13 December 2010, Volume 520.

37. *The Times*, 10 December 2010.

38. Caroline Hoefferle, *British Student Activism in the Long Sixties* (New York: Routledge, 2012), p. 115.

39. *Guardian*, 25 February 1984.

40. *The Sun*, 11 December 2010.

41. Hansard, Public Order Policing, Christopher Pincher (Cons), 13 December 2010, Volume 520.

42. Rosie Bergzoni, 'Kettled During 9th of December Protest', *Indymedia UK*, 10 December 2010.

43. Solomon and Palmieri (eds), *Springtime: The New Student Rebellions*, p. 38.

44. Hansard, Public Order Policing, Theresa May, Secretary of State for the Home Department, 13 December 2010, Volume 520.

45. *The Sun*, 11 December 2010.

46. Hansard, Public Order Policing, Theresa May, Home Secretary, 13 December 2010, Volume 520.

47. Hansard, Public Order Policing, Ed Balls, Shadow Home Secretary, 13 December 2010, Volume 520.

48. Ibid. Jeremy Corbyn (Lab).

49. Ibid. Robert Halfon (Con).

50. *Guardian*, 11 December 2010.

51. Hansard, Public Order Policing, Duncan Hames (Lib), 13 December 2010, Volume 520.

52. Solomon and Palmieri (eds), *Springtime: The New Student Rebellions*, p. 29.

53. Ibid.

54. Jody McIntyre interview, BBC News Channel, 8 o'clock News, 13 December 2010.

5   *Occupy, Agitate, Organise*

1. Mason, *Why It's Kicking Off Everywhere*, p. 44.

2. Ibid.

3. Feyzi Ismail, 'The Politics of Occupation', in Michael Bailey and Des Freedman (eds), *The Assault on Universities: A Manifesto of Resistance* (London: Pluto, 2011).

4. R. Rheingans and R. Hollands, 'There is No Alternative?': Challenging Dominant Understandings of Youth politics in Late Modernity Through a Case Study of the 2010 UK Student Occupation Movement', *Journal of Youth Studies*, 16:4 (2013), pp. 546–64.

5. Cockburn and Blackburn (eds), *Student Power*, pp. 7–21.

6. Owen Hatherley, 'The Occupation of Space', in Hancox (ed.), *Fight Back! A Reader on the Winter of Protest*, p. 121.

7. Jonathan Moses, 'Postmodernism in the Streets: The Tactics of Protest are Changing', in Hancox (ed.), *Fight Back! A Reader on the Winter of Protest*, pp. 88–92.

8. *Independent*, 8 February 2009.

9. Ibid.

10. Hugo Rifkind, 'Angry Young Things', *The Times*, 16 February 2009.

11. Dario Azzellini and Maria Sitrin, *They Can't Represent Us! Reinventing Democracy from Greece to Occupy* (London: Verso, 2014).

12. Patrick Kingsley, 'G2: Power to the Pupils: Students Have Been Staging Sit-ins at Campuses Across the UK in Protest Against Education Cuts', *Guardian*, 30 November 2010.

13. Solomon and Palmieri (eds), *Springtime: The New Student Rebellions*, p. 71.

14. Fraser, *1968: A Student Generation in Revolt*, p. 250.

15. Kingsley, 'G2: Power to the Pupils'.

16. Danny Hayward, 'Adventures in the Sausage Factory: A Cursory Overview of UK University Struggles, November 2010–July 2011', *Metamute Journal*, 25 January 2012.

17. Antonio Negri, *Books for Burning: Between Civil War and Democracy in 1970s Italy* (London: Verso, 2005).

18. Nanni Balestrini, *The Unseen* (London: Verso, 1989). The novel covers the experience of Autonomia in late 1970s Italy through the eyes of a young protagonist.

19. *Guardian*, 30 November 2010.

20. Lee Salter and Jilly Boyce Kay, 'The UWE Student Occupation', *Social Movement Studies*, 10:4 (2011), pp. 423–9.

21. Ibid.

22. Yannis Theocharis, 'Cuts, Tweets, Solidarity and Mobilisation: How the Internet Shaped the Student Occupations', *Parliamentary Affairs*, 65 (2012), pp. 162–94.

23. Ibid.

24. Manuel Castells, *Networks of Outrage and Hope: Social Movements in the Internet Age*, (London: Polity, 2012), p. 11.

25. Kristin Ross, *May '68 and Its Afterlives* (Chicago: Chicago University Press, 2002), p. 8.

26. *Guardian*, 9 December 1971.

*6 Why Did the Students Lose?*

1. *Guardian*, 9 December 2010.

2. Ibid.

3. *The Times*, 11 November 2010.

4. Aaron Porter talks at UCL Occupation, 28 November 2010, https://www.youtube.com/watch?v=qpRCDmhhgrg.

5. *Guardian*, 7 December 2010.

6. *Bath Chronicle*, 10 December 2010.

7. *Guardian*, 24 November 2010.

8. *Guardian*, 21 December 2010.

9. Barnett, 'Student Power: 1968 ... 2010'. See also 'Failure of the 2010 UK Student Movement: A Diagnosis', Novara FM (podcast), 1 November 2013, http://novaramedia.com/2013/11/failure-of-the-2010-uk-student-movement-a-diagnosis.

10. *Guardian*, 27 November 2010.

11. E.P. Thompson, *Out of Apathy* (London: Stevens & Sons, 1960), and Robin Archer (ed.), *Out of Apathy: Voices of the New Left 30 Years On* (London: Verso, 1989).

12. YouGov, 'The Student Vote', 30 November 2010, http://ukpollingreport.co.uk/blog/archives/2894.

13. Younge, 'Students are Not Revolting'.

14. *Guardian*, 11 November 2010.

15. YouGov, 'YouGov on Woolas and the Tuition Fees Protests', for *The Sunday Times*, 24 November 2010, http://ukpollingreport.co.uk/blog/archives/2874.

16. Dave Lyddon, 'The Changing Pattern of UK Strikes, 1964–2014', *Employee Relations*, 37:6 (2015), pp. 733–45.

17. *Guardian*, 13 November 2010.

18. 'Student Protests: Downing Street Condemns Lecturers', BBC News, 12 November 2010, http://www.bbc.co.uk/news/uk-politics-11745570.

19. Len McCluskey, 'Unions Get Set for Battle', *Guardian*, 19 December 2010.

20. Biggs, 'At the Occupation', *London Review of Books*.

## Conclusion

1. *Financial Times*, 11 December 2010.

2. *Guardian*, 9 December 2010.

3. Yanis Varoufakis, 'Yanis Varoufakis Full Transcript: Our Battle to Save Greece', *New Statesman*, 13 July 2015.

4. Ross, *May '68 and Its Afterlives*, p. 3.

5. Kingsley, 'G2: Power to the Pupils'.

6. William Morris, *A Dream of John Ball* (London, 1886), at https://www.marxists.org/archive/morris/works/1886/johnball/johnball.htm.

7. William Davies, 'The New Neoliberalism', *New Left Review*, No. 101, September–October, 2016.

8. YouGov, 'The Student Vote', 30 November 2010.

9. Ibid.

10. Hansard, Higher Education Fees, Greg Mulholland (Lib), 9 December 2010, Volume 520.

11. *Guardian*, 12 November 2010.

12. Hansard, Higher Education Fees, Julian Lewis (Cons), 9 December 2010, Volume 520.

13. *The Times*, 11 November 2010.

14. Younge, 'Students are Not Revolting'.

15. Ibid.

16. Paul Piccone, 'Reinterpreting 1968: Mythology on the Make', *Telos*, 77 (1988), pp. 7–43.

17. Martin Klimke and Joachim Scharloth (eds), *1968 in Europe: A History of Protest and Activism, 1956–1977* (New York: Palgrave Macmillan, 2009), p. 7.

18. Alexander Hensby, 'Networks of Non-Participation: Comparing "Supportive", "Unsupportive" and "Undecided" Non-Participants in the UK Student Protests Against Fees and Cuts', *Sociology*, online first, 13 October 2015.

19. Ibid.

20. Frantz Fanon, 'On National Culture', in M. Asante (ed.), *African Intellectual Heritage: A Book of* Sources (Philadelphia: Temple University Press, 1996), p. 236.

21. *Guardian*, 4 October 2016.

22. *Guardian*, 21 March 2014.

23. The Public Accounts Committee, 44th Report, *Student Loan Repayments*, 14 February 2014.

24. *Guardian*, 1 August 2016.

25. Lord Baker of Dorking (Chair), 'The Skills Mismatch', The Edge Foundation, 2014, http://www.edge.co.uk/media/130721/the_skills_mismatch_march_2014_final.pdf.

26. Stephen Kemp-King, 'The Graduate Premium: Manna, Myth or Plain Mis-selling?', The Intergenerational Foundation, August 2016.

27. Higher Education Careers Services Unit (HECSU), 'What do Graduates Do?', September 2013, http://www.hecsu.ac.uk/assets/assets/documents/WDGD_sept_2013.pdf

28. UCAS Analysis and Research, End of Year Report, December 2016.

29. *The Economist*, 3 March 2016.

30. 'My Student Loan was Mis-sold, Says Graduate', BBC News, 26 May 2016, http://www.bbc.co.uk/news/education-36388011.

31. *Guardian*, 9 December 2010.

32. *Guardian*, 16 November 2016.

33. Ibid.

34. *Guardian*, 17 September 2016.

35. *Guardian*, 15 November 2016.

36. Ibid.

37. Ibid.

38. Mason, *Why It's Kicking Off Everywhere*, p. 62.

39. François Furet, *Interpreting the French Revolution* (Cambridge: Cambridge University Press, 1981), pp. 5–6.

40. Daniel Cohn-Bendit, *Forget 68* (Paris: Editions de l'Aube, 2008).

41. 'Nous en avons pris la flamme, vous n'en avez gardé que la cendre.' Jean Jaurès, January 1910, in a speech made in Paris at the Chamber of Deputies, cited in Jean Jaurès, *Pages choisies de Jean Jaurés* (Paris: Rieder, 1922), p. 115.

# Bibliography

*Books and theses*

Aldrich, R. (ed.), *A Century of Education* (London: Routledge, 2002).

Archer, R. (ed.), *Out of Apathy: Voices of the New Left 30 Years On* (London: Verso, 1989).

Ashby, E. and Anderson, M., *The Rise of the Student Estate in Britain* (London: Macmillan and Co Ltd, 1970).

Azzellini, D. and Sitrin, M., *They Can't Represent Us! Reinventing Democracy from Greece to Occupy* (London: Verso, 2014).

Bailey, M. and Freedman, D. (eds), *The Assault on Universities: A Manifesto of Resistance* (London: Pluto, 2011).

Balestrini, N., *The Unseen* (London: Verso, 1989).

Benjamin, W., *Selected Writings, Vol. 2, Part 2 (1931–1934)* (Cambridge, MA: Harvard University Press, 2005).

Bourdieu, P., *Firing Back: Against the Tyranny of the Market* (London: New Press, 2003).

Brewis, G., *A Social History of Student Volunteering: Britain and Beyond, 1880–1980* (Basingstoke: Palgrave Macmillan, 2014).

Castells, M., *Networks of Outrage and Hope: Social Movements in the Internet Age* (London: Polity, 2012).

Cockburn, A. and Blackburn, R. (eds), *Student Power* (Harmondsworth: Penguin, 1969).

Cohn-Bendit, D., *Forget 68* (Paris: Editions de l'Aube, 2008).

Cornils, I., and Waters, S. (eds), *Memories of 1968* (Oxford: Peter Lang, 2010).

Cunningham, S. and Lavalette, M., *Schools Out! The Hidden History of Britain's School Student Strikes* (London: Bookmarks, 2016).

Degroot, G. (ed.), *Student Protest: The Sixties and After* (London: Routledge, 1998).

Donnelly, M., *Sixties Britain: Culture, Society, Politics* (London: Routledge, 2005).

Ehrlich, A.Z., *The Leninist Organizations in Britain and the Student Movement 1966–1972*, PhD thesis, University of London, 1981.

Fanon, F., 'On National Culture', in M. Asante (ed.), *African Intellectual Heritage: A Book of Sources* (Philadelphia: Temple University Press, 1996).

Fisher, M., *Capitalist Realism* (London: Zero Books, 2009).

Fox, S., *Apathy, Alienation and Young People: The Political Engagement of British Millennials*, PhD thesis, University of Nottingham, 2015.

Fraser, R., *1968: A Student Generation in Revolt* (London: Pantheon, 1988).

Furet, F., *Interpreting the French Revolution* (Cambridge: Cambridge University Press, 1981).

Gildea, R., Mark, J. and Warring, A. (eds), *Europe's 1968: Voices of Revolt* (Oxford: Oxford University Press, 2013).

Gluck, S-B. and Patai, D. (eds), *Women's Words: The Feminist Practice of Oral History* (New York: Routledge, 1991).

Grele, R. (eds), *Envelopes of Sound: The Art of Oral History* (Chicago: Precedent Publishing, 1975).

Guerrini, G., *Individualisation and Student Responses to Higher Education Tuition Fees in the UK 1998–2003*, PhD thesis, University of Warwick, 2007.

Hancox, D. (ed.), *Fight Back! A Reader on the Winter of Protest* (London: Open Democracy, 2011).

Hanna, E., *Student Power! The Radical Days of the English Universities* (Cambridge: Cambridge Scholars Publishing, 2013).

Hervé, H. and Rotman, P., *Génération*. 2 vols. (Paris: Seuil, 1987).

Hobsbawm, E., *On History* (London: Abacus, 1999).

Hoefferle, C.M., *British Student Activism in the Long Sixties* (New York: Routledge, 2013).

Janin, H., *The University in Medieval Life, 1179–1499* (Jefferson: McFarland and Company, 2008).

Jarausche, K. (ed.), *The Transformation of Higher Learning, 1860–1930* (Chicago: Chicago University Press, 1982).

Jaurès, J., *Pages choisies de Jean Jaurés* (Paris: Rieder, 1922).

Klimke, M. and Scharloth, J. (eds), *1968 in Europe: A History of Protest and Activism, 1956– 1977* (New York: Palgrave Macmillan, 2009).

Kumar, A., *'Did We Achieve Anything': Evaluating the Effectiveness of the 2010 UK Student Protests*, LSE MSc thesis, 2011, http:// www.academia.edu/3722137/_Did_We_Change_Anything_ Evaluating_the_Effectiveness_of_the_2010_UK_Student_ Protests.

Lawton, D., *Education and Labour Party Ideologies 1900–2001 and Beyond* (London: Routledge, 2005).

Luxemburg, R., *Reform or Revolution* and *The Mass Strike* (Chicago: Haymarket, 2008).

Mair, P., *Ruling the Void: The Hollowing of Western Democracy* (London: Verso, 2013).

Malik, S., *The Jilted Generation* (London: Icon Books, 2010).

Mannheim, K., *Karl Mannheim: Essays on the Sociology of Knowledge* (London: Routledge & Kegan Paul, 1972).

Marwick, A., *The Sixties: Cultural Revolution in Britain, France, Italy, and the United States, c.1958–c.1974* (Oxford: Oxford University Press, 1998).

Mason, P., *Why It's Kicking Off Everywhere: The New Global Revolutions* (London: Verso, 2012).

Morris, W., *A Dream of John Ball* (London, 1886), https://www. marxists.org/archive/morris/works/1886/johnball/johnball. htm

Negri, A., *Books for Burning: Between Civil War and Democracy in 1970s Italy* (London: Verso, 2005).

Parkin, F., *Middle Class Radicalism: The Social Bases of* the British Campaign for Nuclear Disarmament (Manchester: Manchester University Press, 1968).

Passerini, L., *Autobiography of a Generation* (Middletown: Wesleyan University Press, 1996).

Portelli, A., *The Battle of Valle Giulia: Oral History and the Art of Dialogue* (Wisconsin: University of Wisconsin Press, 1997).

Ritchie, D., *Doing Oral History: A Practical Guide* (Oxford: Oxford University Press, 2014).

Rooke, M., *Anarchy and Apathy: Student Unrest 1968–1970* (London: Hamish Hamilton, 1971).

Ross, K., *May '68 and Its Afterlives* (Chicago: Chicago University Press, 2002).

Samuel, R. and Thompson, P., *The Myths We Live By* (London and New York: Routledge, 1990).

Seel, B., Patterson, M. and Doherty, B. (eds), *Direct Action in British Environmentalism* (London: Routledge, 2000).

Solomon, S. and Palmieri, T. (eds), *Springtime: The New Student Rebellions* (London: Verso 2011).

Thompson, E.P., *Out of Apathy* (London: Stevens & Sons, 1960).

Thompson, E.P. (ed.), *Warwick University Ltd* (London: Spokesman Books, 1970).

Thompson, E.P., *The Making of the English Working Class* (Harmondsworth: Penguin, 2013).

Thompson, P., *Voice of the Past* (Oxford: Oxford University Press, 1979).

Webster, S.L., *Protest Activity in the British Student Movement, 1945 to 2011*, PhD thesis, Manchester University, 2015.

Willetts, D., *The Pinch: How the Baby Boomers Took Their Children's Future – And Why They Should Give it Back* (London: Atlantic Books, 2011).

Wohl, R., *Generation of 1914* (Cambridge, MA: Harvard University Press, 1979).

*Journal articles*

Alexander, H., 'Networks of Non-Participation: Comparing "Supportive", "Unsupportive" and "Undecided" Non-Participants in the UK Student Protests against Fees and Cuts', *Sociology*, online first, 13 October 2015.

Backman, E. and Finlay, D., 'Student Protest: A Cross-National Study', *Youth and Society*, 5 (1973–4).

Barker, C., 'Some Reflections on Student Movements of the 1960s and Early 1970s', *Revista Crítica de Ciências Sociais*, 81 (2008).

Benn, R. and Fieldhouse R., 'Government Policies on University Expansion and Wider Access, 1945–51 and 1985–91 Compared', *Studies in Higher Education*, 18:3 (2003).

Biggs, J., 'At the Occupation', *London Review of Books*, 16 December 2010.

Burkett, J., 'The National Union of Students and Transnational Solidarity, 1958–1968', *European Review of History*, 21 (2014).

Clark, H., 'Youth Participation: Creating Good Citizens or Good Subjects?', *Anthropology Matters*, 10:1 (2008).

Collini, S., 'Browne's Gamble', *London Review of Books*, 4 November 2010.

Collini, S., 'Sold Out', *London Review of Books*, 24 October 2013.

Crossley, N., 'Social Networks and Student Activism: On the Politicizing Effect of Campus Connections', *The Sociological Review*, 56:1 (2008).

Davies, W., 'The New Neoliberalism', *New Left Review*, 101, September–October 2016.

Giguere, B. and Lalande, R., 'Why Do Students Strike? Direct and Indirect Determinants of Collective Action Participation', *Political Psychology*, 31 (2010).

Grele, R., 'Listen to Their Voices', *Oral History*, 7 (1979).

Gross, M., 'Bologna Resistance', *Current Biology*, 20:2 (2010).

Hanna, E., 'The English Student Movement: An Evaluation of the Literature', *Sociology Compass*, 2:5 (2008).

Hayward, D., Adventures in the Sausage Factory: A Cursory Overview of UK University Struggles, November 2010–July 2011', *Metamute Journal*, 25 January 2012.

Ibrahim, J., 'The New Toll of Higher Education and the UK Student Revolts of 2010–2011', *Social Movement Studies*, 10:4 (2011).

Ibrahim, J., 'The Moral Economy of the UK Student Protest Movement 2010–2011', *Contemporary Social Sciences*, 9:1 (2014).

Levine, A. and Wilson, K., 'Student Activism in the 1970s: Transformation Not Decline', *Higher Education*, 8 (1979).

Lyddon, D., 'The Changing Pattern of UK Strikes, 1964–2014', *Employee Relations*, 37:6 (2015).

Passerini, L., 'Work Ideology and Consensus Under Italian Fascism', *History Workshop*, 8 (Autumn 1979).

Piccone, P., 'Reinterpreting 1968: Mythology on the Make', *Telos*, 77 (1988).

Rheingans, R. and Hollands, R., '"There is No Alternative?": Challenging Dominant Understandings of Youth politics in Late Modernity Through a Case Study of the 2010 UK Student Occupation Movement', *Journal of Youth Studies*, 16:4 (2013).

Salter, L. and Kay, J-B., 'The UWE Student Occupation', *Social Movement Studies*, 10:4 (2011).

Samuel, R., 'Perils of Transcript', *Oral History*, 1:2 (1971).

Simon, B., 'The Student Movement in England and Wales During the 1930s', *History of Education*, 16:3 (1987).

Sirinelli, J-F., 'Génération, générations', *Vingtième Siècle. Revue d'histoire*, No. 98 (2008).

Theocharis, Y., 'Cuts, Tweets, Solidarity and Mobilisation: How the Internet Shaped the Student Occupations', *Parliamentary Affairs*, 65 (2012).

Thomas, N., 'Challenging Myths of the 1960s: The Case of Student Protest in Britain', *Twentieth Century British History*, 13:3 (2002).

E.P. Thompson, 'The Moral Economy of the English Crowd in the 18th Century', *Past & Present*, 50 (February 1971).

Yow, V., '"Do I Like Them Too Much?" Effects of the Oral History Interview on the Interviewer and Vice-Versa', *Oral History Review*, 24:1 (Summer 1997).

*Newspapers, websites and think tanks*

Afterall Online
*Bath Chronicle*
BBC News website
*Birmingham Mail*
*Burnley Express*
*Daily Mail*
*Daily Post* (Liverpool)
Deterritorial Support Group website
*Evening Standard*
*Exeter Express and Echo*

*Financial Times*
*Gloucestershire Echo* (Cheltenham)
Higher Education Careers Services Unit (HECSU)
*Il Manifesto*
Indymedia UK
*International Times*
k-punk blog
Lenin's Tomb blog
*Liverpool Echo*
*Monthly Review*
*Morning Star*
New Left Project
*New Society*
*New Statesman*
NUS Research Publications
Open Democracy online
*Oxford Mail*
*South Wales Echo*
The Edge Foundation
*The Gazette*
*The Guardian*
The Intergenerational Foundation
*The Irish Times*
The Opinion Panel Research
*The Scotsman*
*The Sun*
*The Times*
UCAS Analysis and Research
*Western Daily Press*
*Yorkshire Post*
YouGov

*Film, television and video*

Aaron Porter talks at UCL Occupation, 28 November 2010, https://www.youtube.com/watch?v=qpRCDmhhgrg.

BBC Jody McIntyre interview, BBC News Channel, 13 December 2010, https://www.youtube.com/watch?v=tXNJ3MZ-AUo.

BBC *Newsnight*, 9 December 2010, 'Paul Mason reports on tuition fees protest', https://www.youtube.com/watch?v=-vfINMJBwcU.

Lethal Bizzle – Pow – Rave in Parliament Square, London – Anti Cuts Protest X3 – 09/12/10, https://www.youtube.com/watch?v=WFDobI7CqNA.

*Night and Fog in Japan*, dir. Nagisa Oshima, Japan, Shochiku, 1960.

Novara Media, 'Failure of the 2010 UK Student Movement: A Diagnosis', Novara FM (podcast), Season 3, Episode 9, 1 November 2013, http://novaramedia.com/2013/11/failure-of-the-2010-uk-student-movement-a-diagnosis.

*The Real Social Network*, dir. Ludovica Fales and Srdjan Keca, London, 2012.

*Parliamentary records and archives*

David Cameron, Prime Minister's Speech on Education, 8 December 2010, Cabinet Office, CentreForum, https://www.gov.uk/government/speeches/pms-speech-on-education.

David Willetts, Oral Statement to Parliament, Universities UK Spring Conference 2011, 25 February 2011, https://www.gov.uk/government/speeches/universities-uk-spring-conference-2011.

Dearing Report, *Higher Education in the Learning Society*, London: HMSO, 1997.

Department for Business, Innovation and Skills, *Putting Students at the Heart of the System*, Higher Education report, June 2011.

Hansard, Higher Education Fees, 9 December 2010, Volume 520.

Hansard, Public Order Policing, 13 December 2010, Volume 520.

Liberal Democrat Manifesto 2010.

'Letter from Straw to Executive', 8 December 1971, Modern Records Centre, Warwick University, MSS.280/50/3.

Lord Browne, *An Independent Review of Higher Education Funding and Student*

*Finance in England*, 12 October 2010, National Archives (UK).

# Index